CW00550388

SUNDAY'S SERMON FOR MONDAY'S WORLD

THE GOSPEL AND OUR CULTURE SERIES

A series to foster the missional encounter of the gospel
with North American culture

John R. Franke
Series Editor

•　　•

Recently Published

Michael Barram, *Missional Economics:
Biblical Justice and Christian Formation*

Craig Van Gelder and Dwight J. Zscheile, *Participating in God's Mission:
A Theological Missiology for the Church in America*

Michael W. Goheen, ed., *Reading the Bible Missionally*

Stefan Paas, *Church Planting in the Secular West:
Learning from the European Experience*

Darrell L. Guder, *Called to Witness: Doing Missional Theology*

Michael J. Gorman, *Becoming the Gospel: Paul, Participation,
and Mission*

*For a complete list of published volumes in this series,
see the back of the book.*

Sunday's Sermon for Monday's World

Preaching to Shape Daring Witness

Sally A. Brown

WILLIAM B. EERDMANS PUBLISHING COMPANY

GRAND RAPIDS, MICHIGAN

Wm. B. Eerdmans Publishing Co.
4035 Park East Court SE, Grand Rapids, Michigan 49546
www.eerdmans.com

© 2020 Sally A. Brown
All rights reserved
Published 2020
Printed in the United States of America

26 25 24 23 22 21 20   1 2 3 4 5 6 7

ISBN 978-0-8028-7112-1

Library of Congress Cataloging-in-Publication Data

Names: Brown, Sally A. (Sally Ann), author.
Title: Sunday's sermon for Monday's world : preaching to shape daring witness /
    Sally A. Brown.
Description: Grand Rapids, Michigan : William B. Eerdmans Publishing Com-
    pany, 2020. | Series: The gospel and our culture | Includes bibliographical
    references and index. | Summary: "Equips preachers to design sermons to
    inspire believers to act with improvisational, creative courage in the ordinary
    settings of their Monday-to-Saturday lives"—Provided by publisher.
Identifiers: LCCN 2019044546 | ISBN 9780802871121 (paperback)
Subjects: LCSH: Preaching.
Classification: LCC BV4211.3 .B763 2020 | DDC 251—dc23
LC record available at https://lccn.loc.gov/2019044546

In honor and memory of

Peter Townsend Dunbar
(March 23, 1943–May 10, 2016)
companion of my soul for twenty-nine years

Donald Van Arsdale Brown
(September 29, 1920–July 16, 2016)
my father,
a model of faith, gentleness, and generosity

Contents

Foreword

Preaching may have lost some of its so-called authority over the years, but it has not lost its (trans)formational power. From store-fronts to neogothic liturgical spaces, preaching still lives every Sunday across the globe as sermons travel out from pulpits into the lives and hearts of the listeners in the pews. Even as we continue to hear the mantra "the church is dying," one thing is for sure—the Word of God is not dead. The Word is resurrecting not only in church seats but on society's streets, whether we recognize it or not. Just as Jesus, the living Word, became flesh and lived among us (John 1), the proclaimed Word takes on our human flesh every Sunday as we witness to the gospel of Jesus Christ every Monday in the world. The Word preached in our sanctuaries is embodied on the streets because the Word cannot be divided, though this may not always be evident.

This means that, as Sally Brown argues, Sunday sermons are a public formational discourse that have public impact as they shape the lives of hearers for "daring witness" in "Monday's world." In the power of the Spirit, Sunday is linked to Monday and the other days of the week, such that there is continuity and congruity between what is preached and what is lived. Truly, the Spirit aims for the integrity of preaching, which means for Christians there is really only one Word in the church and the world: not a Sunday Word and a Monday Word, but an everyday Word, whole and holy.

What this book urges readers to consider is how the sermon is lived as a public witness that testifies "to the radical mercy, inclusive love, and restorative justice of God." In other words, Brown nudges us toward what Saint Augustine would call an "eloquent speech." In his *On Christian Doctrine*, which is considered to be the earliest homiletical textbook, Augustine teaches that "the life of the speaker has greater weight in determining whether he is obediently heard than any grandness of eloquence. . . . [M]any . . . would be benefited if they were to do what they say. . . . [H]is way of living may be, as it were, an eloquent speech."[1] Augustine offers an implicit challenge to speakers to "walk the talk" Sunday to Sunday; the same is true for all hearers of the gospel.

But we, as preachers, are challenged to ponder not only how well we whoop in the pulpit but also how well we help our surrounding communities. We are challenged to view preaching much more holistically, connected to the everyday life of Christian witness, and reflect on how we preach with our lives, not only in creeds but in deeds. In this way, our lives would be the "amen" to the proclamation on our lips,[2] causing Christian preachers to truly reach the height of eloquence with the fusion of our rhetoric with our ethic. Brown, in Augustinian fashion, invites us to see eloquent preaching as a practice, not only in a pulpit but also enfleshed through justice, mercy, and love in the world.

A (trans)formational understanding of preaching does not mean that congregations cannot be malformed. This happens when Christians speak and act in ways that are in opposition to the life and work of Jesus Christ. Of course, malformation may not be totally a sermon's fault because other influences could be at play. Nonetheless, we should be mindful that preaching has caused oppressive terror throughout history. But this historic reality does not negate the grace and good that have flowed from pulpits too. Preaching, indeed, has caused redemptive works of mercy and justice in the world.

This may seem to be too high of a calling for the ministry of

---

1. Saint Augustine, *On Christian Doctrine*, trans. D. W. Robertson Jr. (orig. circa 396–426; Upper Saddle River, NJ: Prentice Hall, 1958), 164–66.
2. In his Lyman Beecher lectures, James Forbes says this was true of Jesus; published as *The Holy Spirit and Preaching* (Nashville: Abingdon, 1999).

preaching—to (trans)form others for "daring witness" in the world. Yet it is high because Jesus is high and lifted up, drawing us into the cruciform hope of God. It is high because preaching should always be a practice of resurrection, lifting others up out of a miry clay. It is high because it is rooted in a deep hope grounded in God's redemptive promises for all of creation. And hope does not disappoint (Rom. 5), which is why preaching continues to happen every Sunday in the power of the Spirit. Preachers continue to hope in God, while in fact preaching is a sign that God still has hope in the church and has not yet given up on us.

All of this is weighty in nature because life is weighty. Life and death are always in the balance when it comes to ministry, including preaching. All of this is weighty because we are dealing with God's incarnate glory, meaning something holy and heavy is at stake when we preach. Life and death are at stake.

The weight of it all should be obvious from the very beginning of this fantastic book. The dedication page is penned in love to two significant men in Brown's life—her deceased husband and deceased father. Because of this, we know this book is not just another theological and theoretical treatise on preaching. It is a love letter to the saints who have gone home in faith and for a God who offers the gift of redemptive life through the ministry of preaching every Sunday. The dedication page implies that preaching is a matter of life and death. This writing cost Brown something. It squeezed life and love out of her pen such that we get a glimpse of the love, justice, and hope of God in preaching on Sundays for Monday's world. I hope your reading costs you something too, at least the transformation of your preaching *life*.

Luke A. Powery

Acknowledgments

Every author is aware that her creative efforts are group projects, although only a handful of those whose support makes the difference between success and failure know they've been on the team. I am grateful to countless friends and family members, Princeton Theological Seminary colleagues, colleagues in the Academy of Homiletics, and many doctoral students, who discussed the ideas in this book with me (whether they realized it or not) and sparked my interest in authors I might otherwise have bypassed.

Chief among those who "officially" supported this work are Dr. Craig A. Barnes, president of Princeton Theological Seminary, and (now retired) academic dean and wise homiletics colleague, Dr. James F. Kay. They, along with the board of trustees and my colleagues in the Practical Theology Department, generously supported the half-year sabbaticals in 2012, 2014, and 2017 that expedited this work.

In the wake of two utterly unexpected personal losses in May and July of 2016 (indicated on the dedication page of this volume), the vortex of sheer grief, as well as the practical demands that follow life-altering loss, swallowed my energy and attention. This project lay abandoned on a shelf. My particular thanks go to Cleophus J. LaRue, Michael Brothers, Nancy J. Duff, Luke A. Powery, Paul S. Wilson, Ronald J. Allen, Patrick W. T. Johnson, Sonia Waters, Dale Allison, and Dennis Olson, who, at key points, persuaded me that this work still mattered.

Every author needs a few people in her corner who believe in her, regardless of whether she ever publishes another word. I've been blessed with more than my share. To my women friends of many years: bless you. You know who you are. But above all, I give thanks to God for my late husband, Peter Townsend Dunbar, to whom (along with my late father) this book is dedicated. Peter realized only when it was too late to back out that he had married himself to thirty years of cohabiting with half-finished manuscripts greedy for attention; and yet, when they were finished, Peter—with ungrudging grace—was the first to read them. His generosity of spirit shines in his children, Heather and Andrew, whose forbearance toward their endlessly preoccupied, academically minded stepmother knows no bounds.

I greatly appreciate John Franke for his careful reading of my manuscript, and David Bratt at Eerdmans Publishing, who saw the manuscript through its final stages.

If there is one person without whom this book surely could *not* have happened, it is Michael Thomson, who recognized the promise of this work in its earliest stages. His confidence kept me hopeful that I would resume this project when grief loosened its grip, and his patience kept the door of opportunity open.

Sally A. Brown
Princeton, New Jersey

Introduction: Being Christian in Public

One visionary, creative action by one person can reverberate around the world.

On a Thursday evening, December 1, 1955, Rosa Parks—an African American employee in a department store, weary after another workday on her feet, and weary as well of America's racist double standards—refused to comply with the bus driver's request that she give up her seat in the "colored only" section to a white passenger who had been left standing when the last open seat in the white section was filled.

On June 5, 1989, when a column of tanks rolled into Beijing's Tiananmen Square, part of ongoing military action designed to crush a student-led political uprising, an unknown young man took a stand directly in the path of the first tank, shifting his stance each time it tried to maneuver around him.[1]

In May of 1992, after a shell killed twenty-two innocent citizens in a square near his home in Sarajevo, professional musician Vedran Smailovic played his cello for twenty-two days at the site of their deaths. In subsequent weeks and months, Smailovic continued to play, day after day, at sites where shelling, bombs, and sniper fire

---

1. Although London's *Sunday Express* identified the man as a student named Wang Weilin, this could not be independently verified. He continues to be known as "Tank Man." Reports as to Tank Man's fate vary. Some insist that he was executed by the government within two weeks, while others contend that Tank Man escaped to Taiwan. http://www.independent.co.uk/news/world/asia/tiananmen-square-what -happened-to-tank-man-9483398.html.

were taking lives, often choosing to play amid the shambles of once-beautiful buildings bombed into rubble.[2]

Malala Yousafzai was a Pakistani teenager when she began fighting against government threats in her home country of Pakistan to end education for young women. Taliban extremists took over her school bus and attempted to end her life with a bullet to the head when she was fifteen; but Malala survived. In 2014, at age seventeen, she became the youngest winner of the Nobel Peace Prize. She returned to her home country of Pakistan for the first time on March 29, 2018, where education for girls is again universal today.

Many around the world remember the name Rosa Parks. Most adults recall "the cellist of Sarajevo," although very few know his name. At the time of this writing, the "Tank Man" of Tiananmen Square has yet to be conclusively identified. Malala Yousafzai's fight for girls' education around the globe continues.

Lodged in our memories are the images of these creative, courageous witnesses, daring to signify with their bodily presence in contested spaces their belief in powers of justice and hope that cannot be defeated by those who aim to win by force. An African American woman seated resolutely on a city bus; a cellist absorbed in his music amid destroyed buildings; a slight, lone figure silhouetted before a tank; a young Pakistani woman with bandaged head turned toward the camera, smiling as best she can: these women and men chose to act as "agents of [redemptive] interruption."[3]

While only one of the four identifies Christian faith with the choices made, each of these memorable persons chose to act with

2. Bryan Patterson, "A Day Music Saved Our Mortal Souls," *Sunday Herald Sun* (Melbourne, Australia), October 14, 2001, 71. See also https://en.wikipedia.org/wiki/Vedran_Smailovi%C4%87.

3. The phrase "agents of interruption" is used by Charles L. Campbell and Johann H. Cilliers to refer to the role of the preacher as practitioner of the gospel rhetoric of "folly"—a rhetoric that interrupts and destabilizes the fixed rhetoric and power structures of a world that rejects the power of God expressed through the folly of the cross. I will argue in subsequent pages for its extension as a descriptor for the agency of ordinary Christians who act with redemptive, improvisational daring to interrupt scripts of abusive power in its many forms in the settings and situations of ordinary life. See Charles L. Campbell and Johann H. Cilliers, *Preaching Fools: The Gospel as a Rhetoric of Folly* (Waco, TX: Baylor University Press, 2011), 154.

ingenuity, vision, and purpose amid situations fraught with tension. In doing so, they risked their futures—even their lives.

Rethinking Public Christian Witness for Our Time

A half century or more from now, the early twenty-first century may be lodged in memory as that period in which terrorist tactics became established, domestically and internationally, as a staple of the daily news. In the United States, as elsewhere in the world, reports of acts of terroristic violence are as common an item on the evening newscast as erratic shifts in the price of oil—so common, in fact, that the stock market reacts more sharply, by far, to the latter than to the former. This winter and spring, so many school shootings have taken place that, in the course of table conversation in the cafeteria, I found myself having to ask the person next to me, "Excuse me, which school shooting are we talking about right now?"

In the United States, how safe you are walking down your own street depends, in part, on the color of your skin. In countries around the world, minority ethnic or religious populations are targeted for systematic harassment, deportation, or elimination. Western or "westernized" sociocultural spaces in the twenty-first century are characterized, increasingly, by polarized politics, huge disparities between the well-to-do and the just-getting-by, and a plethora of cultural-linguistic and religious diversities. These social vectors run straight through nearly all the everyday spaces where the people we preach to earn their living and raise their children, learn and socialize, shop and vote.

Under conditions like these, it takes energy to stay socially and politically engaged. The temptation to retreat into homogenous so-cial enclaves along class, ethnic, or religious lines, or to take refuge in social-media "echo chambers" where the disturbance of difference is filtered out, is ever present. Christians are as tempted as anyone else to take refuge in such artificially homogenous spaces. But can we do so with integrity, in precisely that historical moment when public testimony to the mercy, inclusive love, and restorative justice of God—in deed as well as in word—could not be more crucial?

What kind of public witness to God's ongoing, redemptive engagement with the world is called for under the conditions described here? What kind of daring, everyday countertestimonies to the all-too-easy rhetoric of hate might strategic preaching on our part inspire? In other words, how can individual believers discern and, with imaginative courage, participate in the ongoing, redemptive activity of God in the ordinary settings of their everyday lives, testifying with their lives to the mercy, love, and justice of God?

These questions about public Christian witness in our time raise, in turn, homiletical questions. Precisely what strategies in Christian sermons best equip the men, women, and even children in our pews to take daring action that testifies to the radical mercy, inclusive love, and restorative justice of God, doing so in ways that are creative, agile, and apt to the demands of a given moment? How can we who preach inspire the "ordinary prophets" of our time—those who, in Christ's name, will act in great or small ways as agents of (redemptive) interruption?

My aim in this book is to engage readers in constructing answers to these questions. Part I (chapters 1 and 2) provides a theological and theoretical backdrop for the discussion of homiletical strategies in part II.

In chapter 1, I invite preachers to step aside for the moment from the pressing work of sermon preparation to consider several recent strands in late twentieth- and early twenty-first-century theological conversation that, from different perspectives, seek to describe what Christian public witness looks like for our time. I consider in this chapter three specific approaches that bear upon the question of Christian public witness: (1) the *missional* initiative in theology and ministry practice, with its ecclesiological emphasis on the "sent" nature of the church; (2) the *faithful-practices* initiative in formational practical ecclesiology; and (3) the *postliberal* approach to biblical hermeneutics, with its accent on narrative readings of Scripture.

In the course of the chapter, I consider distinctive features and lasting contributions of each of these strands of theological work but also note significant limitations or gaps in each approach. Toward the end of chapter 1, our viewfinder will focus on the question already stated above: *How can individual Christian believers discern and, with imaginative courage, participate in the ongoing, redemptive activity of God in the ordinary settings of their everyday lives, testifying with their lives to the mercy, love, and justice of God?*

Chapter 2 constructs a model for understanding more deeply the dynamics of creative witness in ordinary situations and the landscape of everyday life itself in which such witness will play out. I argue here that the public witness of ordinary Christian lives will be tactical, shaped by the "foolishness" of the cross, and faithfully improvisational. Such witness interrupts the regimes and routines of this world that diminish human lives and hold both the powerful and the disempowered captive to webs of consumerism, mistrust of the "other," entrenched racism, and forms of power that dominate and threaten.

Strategic Preaching to Support Everyday Lives of Daring Witness

Part II consists of four chapters that answer, from different angles, the homiletical question, What particular preaching strategies best support the imaginative, improvisational testimony of Christian lives to the reign of God in the culturally hybrid spaces of everyday life? The four preaching tasks these chapters address include: (1) building **a vision-shaping hermeneutic of promise** into our preaching; (2) building among listeners a deeper reservoir of embodied wisdom by preaching about our **communal, congregational practices**—both those internal to congregational life and those in which we turn outward to engage the spiritual and physical needs of the communities we serve; (3) drawing listeners into **stories, biblical and contemporary**, in such a way that they become for listeners **imaginative "rehearsal" spaces** for action in the world; and (4) handing the listeners the **indispensable tool of metaphorical vision** by which to discern the ongoing, redemptive activity of the Spirit in those ordinary spaces where they work, learn, shop, socialize, and vote. No doubt there are many ways to equip sermon listeners to undertake daringly imaginative, improvisational, faith-anchored action; but I am persuaded that these four in particular are indispensable.

My hope is that these chapters will inspire both preachers and those who listen to them to move from sanctuary to street, week after week, eager to discern and participate in the ongoing, redemptive work of God already underway amid the ordinary scenes and settings of their Monday-to-Saturday lives. It is a world filled with tension and mistrust, widening economic disparities, and tense racial and class divides, to be sure; but it is a world hungry, as well, for the radical mercy, inclusive love, and restorative justice of God. Above all, it is a world alive with redemptive possibility, because there is no place where the Spirit of God is not already present and active, inviting our participation in what God is doing in every place to make all things new.

PART I

Rethinking the Shape of Christian Witness in Everyday Life

Public Witness: Why the Testimony of Individual Christians in Everyday Spaces Still Matters

I was presiding at a wedding in the main sanctuary of the church I had served for thirteen years when I made a discovery: the way "the public" regards the worship rites of religious communities in our society has changed. Once upon a time, all Protestant churches talked about "public" worship—and it really was public. It wasn't surprising to see nonmembers in a service—visitors from out of town, whether visiting family or not, and from time to time, the curious.

But what struck me as the processional music started up and the first bride's attendant started in my direction is that religious worship services, even Christian ones that *still* think of themselves as "public," are regarded less and less as truly "public" by the general population. Instead, in the minds of many people, Christian worship rites—even wedding services—occupy a social zone somewhere between the public and the private. This realization struck me the moment I stepped to the center of the chancel and assessed the size of the congregation. I knew the family was expecting upward of two hundred people at the wedding reception that afternoon; yet barely eighty looked back at me from the pews. It dawned on me that I was seeing this more and more. These days, for more and more people, "going to a wedding" means showing up for the food, the drinks, and the dancing. The wedding service itself is regarded as mostly a family-and-close-friends' affair; for everybody else, attending the religious service, if there is one at all, is strictly optional.

The loss of the truly "public" dimension of "Christian public worship" extends considerably beyond weddings. Long gone—at least in most parts of North America and most assuredly in Europe—are the days when going to public worship was a normal feature of the weekly schedule of those who identified themselves, at least loosely, as "Christian." Very far gone are the days when prominent preachers' sermons were regarded as "public" discourses. The sermons of a city's most prominent preachers might make it, at least in abbreviated form, into Monday's newspaper. (For that matter, the daily newspaper itself has gone the way of the fountain pen and the hand-written party invitation.) True, much more of the preaching we do is publicly available now; many churches post their sermons on their websites. Undoubtedly, persons who profess other faiths, or no faith at all, click on these postings and either listen to them or read them. It would be interesting to know how many of these virtual passersby stick with it all the way to the end. Most hits, on most websites, last ten to twenty seconds.[1]

The cultural shifts that have made religious communities' ostensibly "public" worship services far less "public," in the minds of many, raise a question for those of us who want to make the news of God's mercy and justice, expressed in Jesus Christ, more available: If the credibility of Christian faith no longer depends on the sermons we preach in our "public" worship services, on what *does* the credibility of Christian faith depend? The answer seems obvious. If Christian faith is going to have any persuasive appeal for the religiously uncommitted, that appeal will depend on what Christians say and do *outside* their church buildings in their Monday-to-Saturday lives, in those truly public spaces where they work, learn, exercise, socialize, and volunteer, shoulder-to-shoulder with persons who embrace other faiths or none.

Efforts to make our worship services and other programs welcoming and appealing to those without religious affiliation are laudable. To some degree, these efforts do draw seekers and newcomers into our worship spaces. But we may be considerably overestimating the likelihood that those who profess no religious affiliation,

---

1. See https://www.nngroup.com/articles/how-long-do-users-stay-on-web-pages/.

or who indicate on surveys that they are finished with organized religion, are going either to stumble over our website or drive by the sign announcing our sermon title, resolve to get up, dress up, and show up at church next weekend—and then actually follow through. Maybe. Maybe not.

None of this is news to scholars working in the fields of theology, ecclesiology, and mission. One robust, scholarly and pastoral response to the shifting relationship between Christian congregations and their surrounding communities has coalesced under the banner head of *missional* theology. This initiative involves a rethinking of ecclesial life, both theologically and practically. At its core is the insight that Christian communities, rather than expecting the public to come to them, are intended to go to the public. Rather than being designed primarily to host warm gatherings of the already-committed and the eagerly seeking on a Saturday night or Sunday morning, congregations need to be designed in such a way that they are turned decisively outward, functioning as the "sent" ambassadors of the redemptive love of a "sending" God.[2]

The emphasis in missional theology falls on the congregation as the basic unit of public Christian witness.[3] The congregation as a whole testifies in its public action to the mercy and justice of God. Yet it will be my contention, in this chapter and those to follow, that the public witness of the church may have at least as much to do with a form of witness that missional theologians, to date, have understressed: the credibility of individual Christians taking creative, faithful action in those ordinary, everyday spaces where they carry out their lives, side by side with those who do not share their faith commitments or understand them. In other words, I contend that for many in our culture, the merit of Christian convictions stands or falls with their most visible and accessible embodiment: namely, the words and actions of ordinary professed Christians in those

2. Readers are encouraged to consult the list of works for further reading at the close of this chapter to engage several significant works in missional theology.

3. This conviction is sounded repeatedly in missional writings. See, for example, Patrick W. T. Johnson, *The Mission of Preaching: Equipping the Community for Faithful Witness* (Downers Grove, IL: InterVarsity Academic, 2015), 104.

everyday spaces where believers and nonbelievers alike work and learn, socialize and shop, volunteer and vote.

If this is true, then pastors and preachers need to be giving much more focused attention to preaching in strategic ways to equip those in the pews to become the agile, credible witnesses they need to be. To be sure, adult education classes and involvement in outward-focused, communal efforts of Christian congregations also have an important role in shaping lives of courageous, creative action in everyday settings. Yet, as nearly every pastor readily admits, the proportion of a congregation that consistently attends adult education is considerably less than those who are present for Sunday's sermon. We can't afford to underestimate the capacity of strategically planned preaching to shape the weekday choices that our listeners will make.

The Preaching Task: What's at Stake?

Most preachers say they care about preaching sermons that jump the gap from Sunday's worship service to the world of Monday and beyond. But some cruising through YouTube videos and church websites reveals a pattern: Many preachers' main strategy for shaping Monday-to-Saturday action on the part of listeners is to hand out plenty of "must," "ought," and "should" toward the end of sermons.[4] Well intended as such moral admonition may be, there are reasons to question its effectiveness. Most seasoned churchgoers have learned to expect this language and have become rather good at distancing themselves from it to a degree. On the whole, the motivational "punch" of the ringing moral admonitions

---

4. A significant and notable exception to the rule is the classic celebratory close of sermons in African American and some Latinx traditions. The sermon closes with ringing affirmations about "what shall be" on the plane of human experience in light of the announcement of divine purpose and activity that the sermon has delivered. Precisely this sort of logic, where speech in the indicative mode ("what is the case") rather than the imperative mode ("what we must do") closes the sermon, will be explored more fully in part II of this book.

we launch into the pews week after week may be considerably less than we hope.

On top of that, preachers can have a somewhat simplified and overly optimistic notion of the degree of "agency" (leverage to undertake action) that those in the pews possess in the settings where they work, learn, and socialize. Truth be told, the everyday spaces where our congregants conduct their daily lives are quite socially and religiously complex. In addition, individuals' degree of power to leverage change in these settings depends on the roles they play there, and the social (or professional) capital they have at their disposal. In some settings, they are leaders; in others, they follow. In other words, everyday life is a complex matrix of constraints as well as opportunities. To put it another way, in most of life's everyday, Monday-to-Saturday spaces, those in our pews are likely to find themselves in the minority, religiously speaking. They are "flying solo." On top of that, in many settings, they may exercise fairly limited leverage to challenge prevailing norms in the places where they work, learn, and socialize. More will be said about this later in this chapter.

Realism about the relative weakness of must/ought/should rhetoric, coupled with a sober assessment of the complexities of the "field of action" that is everyday life these days, suggests that we need to rethink the connection between our preaching strategies and the challenges our listeners actually face when they walk through the doors of the sanctuary and into the street. What can we do in the pulpit that might *really* help them move into the world of Monday and beyond with the courage, imagination, and savvy it may take to testify in action and word to God's mercy and justice?

Before we can get down to the homiletical nitty-gritty of answering this question in part II of this book, some orientation to current theological thinking about the nature of public Christian witness today is in order. In addition, developing a more fine-grained and realistic understanding of the dynamics of the "field of action" that is everyday life can help us better understand our homiletical task.

In the remainder of this chapter, we address this question: How might we better understand what public Christian witness looks like, theologically and practically, amid the religiously plural and socially complex landscapes of today's Western and westernized societies? In the next chapter, we'll appropriate the insights of social historians and theorists of human action to better understand the "field of action" that is everyday life. First, we'll explore the "politics"—that is, the power dynamics, constraints, and opportunities—of everyday life settings. Then we will consider some fresh thinking about the role imagination and improvisation may play when individual Christians in ordinary situations seek to testify, in action and in word, to the mercy and justice of the God they've come to know through their faith in Jesus Christ.

Rethinking the Nature and Mission of the Church in a Changing World

These days, dozens of scholars and ecclesiastical leaders around the globe are rethinking the nature of public Christian witness. This rethinking, which began in the late twentieth century, continues to unfold not so much a *single* theological conversation as an array of concurrent and overlapping ones. In the pages to follow, I will invite readers to listen in on three of these scholarly and pastoral conversations, in particular, distinguished from one another by their dominant perspective, yet in some ways mutually reinforcing.[5] After describing the basic contours and commitments of these three projects, we'll consider how they've influenced each other. Finally, we'll take stock of their lasting contributions, as well as possible weaknesses or underdeveloped themes.

This overview will set the backdrop for chapter 2, where the

---

5. My focus here will be on strands of scholarship that practice *faith seeking understanding* in a mode of culturally and historically critical reflection on the canonical Christian Scriptures. Any discussion of the shape of Christian witness today is necessarily limited by one's own social location. I approach my work as a female, ordained pastor of the Presbyterian Church (U.S.A.), teaching in a seminary rooted in the Reformed tradition. Yet this teaching context includes an ever-widening array of denominational and nondenominational worship traditions; its students and faculty are diverse in race and ethnicity, as well as theological perspective and worship practice.

focus is on the nature of action itself in those everyday settings where our sermon listeners work, learn, raise families, socialize, volunteer, and vote.

Missional Theology and Christian Public Witness: A Brief Overview

The first of the three theological projects we'll consider is what is sometimes called the *missional initiative*. Scholars and church leaders who identify with this theological perspective redescribe the nature and mission of the church as *missional*. Since the emergence of the missional movement from robust scholarly conversations on both sides of the Atlantic in the late twentieth century, the language of the movement has suffered a loss of clarity in some sectors, thanks to its popularity. In other words, church leaders of all stripes have readily picked up missional lingo but have sometimes done so without taking fully into account the deeper theological commitments of the crafters of missional thought.

Missional theology emerged in the early 1990s out of a theological conversation among primarily English-speaking, white male theologians in Britain and the United States, many of whom identified in some way with the Reformed stream of theology and worship practice. Two decades later, its core ideas were being energetically appropriated and adapted by working pastors and church leaders across a wider array of denominational and nondenominational churches, although the scholarly conversation continued to be dominated by white male scholars—issues we will touch upon later in this chapter.

The conversation that came to be known as *missional theology* or *the missional initiative* was an effort to wrestle, theologically and practically, with the implications of massive sociocultural shifts that were changing dramatically the role of churches in wider culture and raising questions about the nature and effectiveness of their witness. Most notably, the "alliance" between Christian churches' perspectives on human flourishing and the views of the wider culture had clearly broken down. This shift caused some, albeit not all, missional thinkers to begin speaking of the "post-Christendom" status of the church.[6] Yet regardless of how one named the growing disjunction between the vision and mission of the churches, on one hand, and wider cultural aspirations and norms, on the other, it was clear that the implications for Christian public witness were profound.

Thus, the fresh thinking that began to emerge from the ongoing conversations on both sides of the Atlantic converged around the connection between the nature of God as a "sending" God and the church as a "sent" community. This meant that the "post-Christendom" church ought not to be a refuge *from* the wider cultural scene, but a source of outward-directed witness to the Triune God whose nature is to move *toward* the world in mercy and justice, a movement distilled most fully in the ministry, death, and resurrection of Jesus Christ.

The first set of programmatic missional proposals took shape as a collection of essays, *Missional Church: A Vision for the Sending of the Church*, published in 1998.[7] Since then, the term *missional* has been used and adopted by both scholars and pastors, although—particularly at the level of strategic practices of mission—some of the core theological commitments of the missional initiative's founders are left aside. A brief review of these core commitments is in order.[8]

Core Theological Commitments of the Missional Initiative

First, a key theological point of departure for missional thinking is a robustly *Trinitarian* understanding of God's redemptive work in

6. For a robust "post-Christendom" assessment of the changed relationship between church and society, see Stanley Hauerwas, *After Christendom* (Nashville: Abingdon, 1991).

7. See Darrell L. Guder, ed., *Missional Church: A Vision for the Sending of the Church in North America* (Grand Rapids: Eerdmans, 1998). An earlier collection of essays emerged from specific workgroups on gospel, church, and culture. See George Hunsberger and Craig Van Gelder, *The Church between Gospel and Culture: The Emerging Mission in North America* (Grand Rapids: Eerdmans, 1996).

8. See Craig Van Gelder and Dwight J. Zscheile, *The Missional Church in Perspective: Mapping Trends and Shaping the Conversation* (Grand Rapids: Baker Academic, 2011), 47, 48.

the world (the *missio Dei*, or "mission of God"). While the teaching, acts of mercy and justice, death by crucifixion, and resurrection of Jesus Christ are clearly central to God's redemptive work in the world, missional theologians emphasize that redemption is the *ongoing* work of the Triune God—Father/Creator, Son/Word, and Holy Spirit. In other words, redemption is not limited to events of the past, but is an ongoing divine undertaking, reaching toward the horizon of God's promised future. This Trinitarian redemptive activity is the outworking of God's intent that humanity, as well as all created things, should be redeemed and gathered into God's future, the new creation already inaugurated in the resurrection of Jesus Christ.[9] A theological corollary of this conviction about the nature of redemption is what, for many, constitutes the missional initiative's most characteristic affirmation: "God is a 'sending' God."[10]

A second core commitment of missional theology flows directly from this affirmation: The church is the "sent" community of this "sending" God. Thus, much of the work of missional theologians has had to do with giving a fresh account of ecclesiology—an understanding of the nature and mission of the church(es).[11] Missional theologians emphasize that the church's vocation is not primarily to safeguard a changeless orthodoxy of belief or to provide a refuge for huddled believers, their backs turned on the world. On the contrary, to be "church" is to be "sent" and therefore to participate, by the power of the Spirit, in God's ongoing, redemptive mission (the *missio Dei*) in the world. As Christ was sent to be given over to the world for our redemption, so the church as the body of Christ is, in turn, given over to the world, bearing news of God's relentless

9. On the gathering up of all things in the risen Christ, see Ephesians 1:10 and Colossians 1:15–20; see Romans 8:18–23 on the groaning of creation, awaiting its redemption.

10. The original and oft-quoted phrase of David J. Bosch was, "God is a missionary God." *Transforming Mission: Paradigm Shifts in Theologies of Mission* (Maryknoll, NY: Orbis, 2011), 381.

11. While, from a theological standpoint, *the church* is one, it is helpful to think in terms of *churches* so that we are less likely to imagine *the church* in a totalizing fashion—as if everything that is "church" must look and act like the particular, local expression of it with which one is most familiar.

mercy, inclusive love, and restorative justice. Worship is central to every Christian community's shared existence; yet our gathering around the Word read and preached, our baptism in water and Spirit, our nourishment by the body and blood of Christ at the Table, and our prayer and praise all contribute to a momentum that moves us beyond the sanctuary walls and into the wider world.

Third, a close corollary of missional theology's Trinitarian starting point, and perhaps the point most often overlooked in appropriations of its insights, is the conviction that the Spirit of God continues to work redemptively *not only in the church, but also in the wider world.* The church doesn't move from sanctuary to street in order to "bring God" to a God-forsaken landscape; rather, the church scatters into the world to join the work of God *already underway there.* As Craig Van Gelder and Dwight Zscheile note in their illuminating 2011 retrospective on missional thought and practice, "The church does not have exclusive possession of God's presence and activity. All persons, made in God's image, are born to serve as co-creative creatures with God in the world."[12] The Spirit is at work beyond the church's walls and outside its membership.

A fourth core missional commitment, and one that links it to communities of concern beyond the church, is that God's mission of redemption is broad, embracing the well-being of the whole human person, and reaching as well into nonhuman creation. Scripture's eschatological promise of a redeemed creation and humanity (attested, for example, in Rom. 8:17–23) sets the wide horizon of the church's witness and the broad embrace of its hope.

Consequences for Understanding Christian Public Witness

These core commitments have important consequences for the way we understand the nature of Christian public witness. Missional theology, as a whole, urges a vision of Christian witness to God's redemptive work, decisively inaugurated in Jesus Christ and continuing in the power of the Spirit, that is: (1) broader than soul-salvation;

12. Van Gelder and Zscheile, *Missional Church in Perspective*, 113.

(2) holistic, addressing the needs of the whole person and human community, as well as the ecosystems of our planet; (3) attentive to the wholeness of not only individual persons, but also human communities (especially marginalized communities with limited access to the goods that make for a thriving life); and (4) necessarily expressed in deed, as well as word.

While particular congregations may discern that the Spirit is leading them to reach into their neighborhoods in traditionally evangelistic ways, missional thought suggests that to make this the *only* form that Christian witness takes is to greatly constrict our understanding of the outworking of God's redemptive purposes. God's redemptive activity, engaging the whole human person and the wholeness of human communities, can be expressed through the efforts of people outside the church and will include efforts that contribute to human beings' physical, emotional, and social well-being and empowerment.

Missional Thought, the Faithful-Practices Initiative, and Postliberal Hermeneutics

Missional theologies have emerged in close dialogue with two other late twentieth-century movements in theology, the *faithful-practices* movement in practical theology and *postliberal* biblical hermeneutics. The influence of these two streams of theological work can be detected in many missional projects.

The Faithful-Practices Approach to the Life of Christian Communities

The *faithful-practices* approach to understanding Christian life and witness focuses, as one might guess, on the shared social practices of Christian congregations. Scholars working on questions about the nature and mission of the church from this angle of vision emphasize that Christian faith gets expressed, consistently and distinctively, by the particular social practices that Christian congregations engage in over time. Such practices include a congregation's worship, its practices of hospitality to neighbor and stranger, its educational and faith-formational practices, its decision-making practices, and so on. Christian faith gives Christian communities' practices a distinctive shape—enough that someone worshiping in a city far from home, even if in a Christian church of another denomination, or even worshiping in another language, would very likely recognize such worship practices as prayer, preaching, congregational or choral song, baptism, and Communion. At the same time, congregations also develop distinctive local practices that are fitting for worship, education, and witness within their particular culture and location.

The faithful-practices perspective was developed primarily by scholars working within the field of practical theology. It gained its early momentum thanks to the labors of two practical theologians in particular, Craig Dykstra (Candler School of Theology at Emory University) and Dorothy Bass (Valparaiso University). Through a series of conferences and publications, Dykstra and Bass steadily widened the faithful-practices discussion to include theologians representing a wide denominational spectrum and many fields of study.[13]

In articulating their theological and theoretical commitments, Dykstra and Bass have drawn, in particular, on the work of moral philosopher Alasdair MacIntyre. In the 1980s, MacIntyre, a Scottish moral philosopher, developed a theory about how moral traditions are constituted and maintained. He proposed that at the heart of any moral tradition's existence and distinctive identity are a set of shared social practices that both articulate and sustain that tradition's vision of the good for human existence. MacIntyre defines a social practice as follows:

> By a "practice" I am going to mean any coherent and complex form of socially established cooperative human activity through which goods

13. Representative publications emerging from the faithful-practices initiative include Dorothy C. Bass, ed., *Practicing Our Faith*, 2nd ed. (San Francisco: Jossey-Bass, 2010); Miroslav Volf and Dorothy C. Bass, eds., *Practicing Theology: Beliefs and Practices in Christian Life* (Grand Rapids: Eerdmans, 2002); and Dorothy C. Bass and Craig Dykstra, eds., *For Life Abundant: Practical Theology, Theological Education, and Christian Ministry* (Grand Rapids: Eerdmans, 2008).

internal to that form of activity are realized in the course of trying to achieve those standards of excellence which are appropriate to, and partially definitive of, that form of activity, with the result that human power to achieve excellence, and human conceptions of the ends and goods involved, are systematically extended.[14]

MacIntyre's description of what counts as a "moral community," as well as his understanding of the way its social practices both articulate and sustain its identity, both map reasonably well onto the ongoing life of the church in the world. Taking this cue, Craig Dykstra and Dorothy Bass adapt MacIntyre's definition of a social practice to describe the sort of distinctive social practices that count as specifically *Christian* practices:

> By "Christian practices" we mean *things Christian people do together over time to address fundamental human needs in response to and in the light of God's active presence for the life of the world.*[15]

Christian practices, according to Dykstra and Bass, (1) "address needs that are basic to human existence as such . . . in ways that reflect God's purposes for humankind"; (2) are "necessarily done with other people, across generations and cultures"; and (3) are epistemologically productive, not only expressing a theological understanding of humanity, creation, and the Triune God, but also actually contributing theologically to a community's understanding of itself, other communities, the redemptive work of God in the world, and the contribution it can make to that work of God.[16]

Essential, community-sustaining Christian practices, according to Dykstra and Bass, include worship practices, like baptism and Communion (the Lord's Supper, or Eucharist), Bible reading and preaching, sharing of common concerns and prayer, affirmations

14. See Alasdair MacIntyre, *After Virtue: A Study in Moral Theory*, 2nd ed. (Notre Dame: University of Notre Dame Press, 1984), 197.

15. Craig Dykstra and Dorothy Bass, "A Theological Understanding of Christian Practices," in Volf and Bass, *Practicing Theology*, 18. Emphasis theirs.

16. Dykstra and Bass, "Theological Understanding of Christian Practices," 21–23.

of faith, and congregational song. (Some of these have overlapping functions; for example, congregational song can be praise, prayer, and proclamation.) At the same time, Christian communities engage in outwardly turned practices that bring Christian faith to expression in public ways. It is at this point that some scholars have combined missional thought and a faithful-practices approach to Christian public witness. For some missional theologians, the language of the faithful-practices initiative provided a way to foreground how a congregation testifies to God's redemptive work not only in verbal witness, but also by way of communal actions that engage those outside the congregation, embodying God's inclusive love, radical mercy, and restorative justice.

A congregation may pursue traditional forms of outreach such as providing seeker-focused events or pastoral support to nonmembers; yet Christian witness also includes creating spaces of radical hospitality for one's neighbors, near and far, especially reaching out to populations neglected by the wider community. A congregation's witness might also include shared social practices, like hosting workshops for persons grieving a major loss, regularly providing volunteer "hosts" at a "winter shelter" for the homeless during the coldest months of the year, or regularly joining other religious groups to maintain an urban gardening project to supply "food-desert" neighborhoods with fresh produce.[17]

Among proponents of the "faithful practices" approach to congregational life, the work of Dykstra and Bass is nuanced by critical reflection on the relationship between a congregation's practices, its sociocultural context, and the important matter of appropriate distribution of power. Some who are attracted to faithful-practices language see this approach as a way of imposing strict conformity to a set of unchanging "disciplines" upon a congregation. This is not the approach Dykstra and Bass commend. It is far more pro-

17. For a significant survey of congregational public practices, see Lois Y. Barrett et al., *Treasure in Clay Jars: Patterns in Missional Faithfulness* (Grand Rapids: Eerdmans, 2004). Each chapter is devoted to a specific congregational case study, focusing on the way a particular congregation-wide practice expresses its sense of missional identity.

ductive to cultivate curiosity about the core practices that shape a community's life and ask what kinds of faith-commitments are being articulated through these core practices. Do these practices cohere with what the congregation professes to believe? What does critical reflection on our most characteristic practices tell us about the distribution and uses of power in our congregation?

Yale theologian Kathryn Tanner cautions that we need to be careful, lest we speak as if Christian practices were utterly and unambiguously distinct from anyone else's practices. Christian practices simply are *not* "purely" Christian. The practices of any Christian community are inevitably cultural hybrids, informed by Christian convictions and habits to be sure, but also recognizably dependent on, and entwined with, the practices of surrounding cultures.[18] In fact, congregations *themselves* are "hybrid" spaces in which an array of cultural norms overlap and sometimes compete. Practices need to be shaped to honor these diversities. Otherwise, a community's patterns of practice will correlate most closely with the assumptions and norms of the congregation's dominant social class(es) and ethnicities. What strikes us as "obviously Christian" may have more to do with unconscious assumptions about what is "appropriate" in the eyes of a dominant class, ethnicity, or cultural group. A mature and healthy congregation's practices, at their best, resonate with that congregation's creed and mission but express, at the same time, the contributions of the diversities of culture, ethnicity, and gender identity present in the congregation as a whole.

Postliberal Approaches to Scripture, Community, and Practice

A second major stream of late twentieth-century theology whose influence can be felt in some missional projects has coalesced around *postliberal* approaches to Scripture reading, Christian identity, and Christian worship and witness. Postliberal theology emphasizes reading Scripture as a unified narrative of God in relationship to

18. Kathryn Tanner, "Theological Reflection and Christian Practices," in Volf and Bass, *Practicing Theology*, 231–32.

humanity, one that shapes the lives of individuals and communities around a distinctive set of practices and produces a distinctive theological "grammar." The designation *postliberal* refers to the repudiation, in this approach, of seeking foundations for faith in a universal notion of reason, the stance toward faith characteristic of *liberal* theological projects. Rather, faith for postliberal theologians is a nonfoundationalist participation in the story Scripture tells.

Postliberal theology has given rise to diverse twentieth-century theological developments and thus is difficult to summarize in a few paragraphs. For present purposes, focusing on an influential hermeneutical principle central to postliberal thought will be most useful, since it illuminates connections between postliberal thought, the faithful-practices project, and missional theology.

Many postliberal theologians share as their hermeneutical point of departure the principle that the Christian canon conveys a single, unified narrative; and it is this narrative that shapes the identity of the church and constitutes the coherence of Christian faith. In other words, say postliberal thinkers, the Christian Scriptures not only can but should be read as a single, unified narrative.

Within postliberal hermeneutics, there are two ways that this narrative canonical unity is understood. Some maintain that the Christian canon is *intrinsically* a single, sustained narrative of the redemptive engagement of God with human beings and all creation. We might call this a "strong" narrativist approach to the Christian canon.[19] Other postliberal thinkers, however, argue that the narrative unity of the Christian canon is a heuristic principle, the result of our *taking* the Christian canon *as* a narrative unity. In other words, this "weak" narrativist reading of the canon acknowledges that the sheer diversity of the materials, themes, portraits of God, and ethical codes we find in Scripture militates against the thesis that the canon is "by nature" a single, unified story that portrays, unequivocally, the nature and acts of God. However, say "weak" postliberal narrativists, the materials, themes, portraits of God, and ethical

19. The work of Stanley Hauerwas comes to mind in this regard. See, for example, *The Peaceable Kingdom: A Primer in Christian Ethics* (Notre Dame: University of Notre Dame Press, 1983).

codes in Scripture can be *construed* as a coherent, overarching narrative when read *by* faith and *for* faith by communities of readers who are willing to give themselves over to the overarching vision that it proposes.[20]

Whatever one takes to be the source of the narrative unity of Scripture, whether as a hermeneutical principle intrinsic to the canon, or a manner of reading that is a core practice of Christian communities, the sense of a unified story of God in relation to humanity correlates well with the conviction of faithful-practices theologians that Scripture implies—or to put it more strongly, requires—a certain kind of community constituted through a specific set of distinctive social practices. This story-formed community is characterized by the specific practices the story entails.

Some missional theologians, too, have readily embraced a post-liberal, narrativist stance toward Scripture, finding it conducive to a missional understanding of the nature and mission of the church. The distinctive community formed by the seamless, overarching story that Scripture tells is sent into the world by God to proclaim and live that story and recruit others into the story and the way of life the story shapes.

Postliberal theologians, like missional theologians, have employed the work of Alasdair MacIntyre; but their particular interest is in the close relationship MacIntyre establishes between a tradition's shared social practices and its community-identifying narratives. MacIntyre contends that a community's distinctive narratives interpret its practices, and vice versa. Its practices and core narratives are mutually interpreting and mutually reinforcing.

Adapting MacIntyre's model to describe the relationship of Christian communities to Christian Scripture is an easy step, especially if one embraces a "strong" version of postliberal narrativist hermeneutics. The (singular) canonical narrative of God, known through Jesus Christ, is understood to sponsor and sustain a specific set of distinctively Christian social practices of worship and

---

20. See Charles L. Campbell, *Preaching Jesus: The New Directions for Homiletical Theology in Hans Frei's Postliberal Theology* (Grand Rapids: Eerdmans, 1997).

public witness. This (univocal) Gospel narrative and the distinctive practices it entails function to interpret and reinforce one another.

A relatively recent scholarly project provides a helpful example here. Boston University School of Theology practical theologian Bryan Stone undertakes a reconstruction of the concept and practice of evangelism for the twenty-first century. Using a postliberal-narrativist approach to the reading of Scripture, Stone reads Scripture as a unified story that entails particular, distinctive practices, including (for Stone) pacifism. Stone's strong postliberal-narrativist linkage between Scripture and the life of the church prompts him to call uncompromisingly for the church to live as a "contrast" community. As it pursues the practices that interpret its identity-conferring narrative, argues Stone, the church's witness both judges and invites the watching world through its manifestation of the reign of God. Evangelism, then, becomes not a specific *practice* of Christian churches among many, but the dynamic *effect* of the church's distinctive life before the world.[21] Stone might well resist Kathryn Tanner's suggestion, noted earlier, that a Christian congregation's practices inevitably betray a significant level of dependency on the practices of its cultural surround.

One can also detect echoes of postliberal thought in the work of some of the early architects of missional thought. For example, Innagrace Dietterich, part of the scholarly consultation in the United States that issued in the initial missional "manifesto," *Missional Church* (1998), states that the purpose of ecclesial communities is "to challenge the world's presuppositions and to offer an alternative perspective of reality *as well as an alternative social*

---

21. Bryan Stone, *Evangelism after Christendom* (Grand Rapids: Brazos, 2007). Notably, Stone, in an aside on the missional movement, writes: "I do not disagree entirely with those theologies of evangelism and mission that urge a shift away from what is disparagingly called 'ecclesiocentrism' to a focus instead on *God's* mission in the world. . . . But if God's calling out of a people is, in fact, the *missio Dei*, then pitting a mission-centered evangelism over against a church-centered evangelism is setting up a false dichotomy" (189). Stone, who identifies aspects of his approach with Hauerwas and John Howard Yoder, undertakes a narrativist-communitarian rethinking of the church, which makes evangelism simply an outgrowth of its life of distinctive practices, not a separate and discrete practice, in and of itself.

order.[22] Developing her description of the "missional community" further, Dietterich cites the work of widely known postliberal theologians Richard B. Hays and Stanley M. Hauerwas, thus implicitly endorsing their characterization of the Christian canon as a univocal narrative.[23]

Postliberal hermeneutics, whether of the "strong" or "weak" variety, seems to partner well with a faithful-practices approach to congregational life and a missional perspective on the public witness of the church. For many, a vision of the church as an alternative social order, or contrast "culture," within a religiously pluralistic society is attractive. At the same time, caution is in order. Missional, faithful-practices, and postliberal models of what it means to bear witness to the redemptive work of God in the world need to be considered critically against lived realities of congregational life and individual Christian experience amid the complexities of multicultural and religiously diverse Western and westernized societies. The next section of this chapter is devoted to evaluating the strengths, but also possible limitations, of the models of congregational life and witness we have described here.

Strengths and Limitations of a Missional Perspective on Christian Witness

In this section, we will first assess some of the chief strengths of a missional approach to Christian witness in today's world. This model of the church can be especially compelling when coupled—as it has been by some proponents of missional theology—with the faithful-practices movement or postliberal, narrativist approaches to Scripture. A bracing simplicity in the picture of Christian faithfulness emerges: We immerse ourselves in the story Scripture tells, we join other believers in consistent, shared social practices throughout the week that cohere with that story, and we move out into the world as transparent, unequivocal witnesses to the redemptive work of God.

22. Innagrace T. Dietterich, "Missional Community," in Guder, *Missional Church*, 149.
23. Dietterich, "Missional Community," 149, 153.

But we will also need to consider, later in this section, whether such a model of Christian life in today's world is realizable and sustainable amid the competing demands of everyday life for most of those in our pews. Might the missional model of public witness be one very useful model for Christian life and witness in the world today, but not sufficient in and of itself to the complexities of twenty-first-century life?

Strengths of a Missional Approach to the Church's Life and Witness

Missional theology, sometimes coupled with postliberal readings of Scripture and a faithful-practices vision of congregational life, has been embraced by pastors and congregations across a broad denominational and theological spectrum. Seeing one's congregation as God's "sent" community for a particular time and place has proven energizing for many churches. Undoubtedly, this understanding of what it means to be "church" in our time has several strengths.

First, the missional movement's vision of the church as a "sent" community has helped many twenty-first-century congregations claim a robust sense of their identity and mission amid a socially and religiously complex cultural landscape. A missional, practice-centered ecclesiology grants congregations a renewed sense of vocation in a world where Christian communities' faith plays a less prominent role in public discourse. A faithful-practices perspective on congregational life can also be a help. When a congregation's identity is centered more fully in its shared, distinctive practices and its "sent" identity, it has a better chance of holding onto its buildings with a less possessive grip, seeing these assets as resources to be shared, rather than private property to be protected from outsiders. Moreover, if a congregation is helped to discern theological continuities between its practices of worship and its practices of witness (a matter we will explore further in chapter 4 of this book), its members are likely to engage all of these practices with a greater sense of purpose.

Second, a missional understanding of congregational life and witness can allow a congregation to see other religious communities as partners rather than competitors—or worse yet, threats. When missional congregations fully embrace the central missional tenet that God works redemptively in the world *through* the church, and yet also works redemptively *beyond* the church, a more generous understanding of the church's relationship with other faith communities can flourish. As Van Gelder and Zscheile put it, "The missional church . . . is a community that constantly looks for the Spirit's leading in its own life and in the surrounding neighborhood," and thus, "its communal imagination must be pregnant with anticipation of the Spirit."[24] This anticipatory imagination helps a congregation move into the weekday world fully confident that they will discern in that landscape evidences of God's redemptive action that invite their participation.

Third, an accent on shared, congregational practices of witness as a crucial form of Christian testimony in the public realm helps congregations reclaim an ecclesiology that is action oriented, relevant, flexible, and revisable. Gone are the days when Christian leaders and congregations were regarded by the wider culture as staunch custodians of dominant cultural values. Such a role for the church no longer works amid the religious and social pluralisms of Western and westernized societies around the world. Missional theology's reorientation of the church's role in relation to public life as one of witness-bearing to the mercy and justice of God, understood through the servanthood of Jesus Christ, replaces public moralism with humble service undertaken with the guidance of the Spirit. The case for the credibility of Christian faith is made through servant-like action in the way of Jesus, not aloof public pronouncement.

The missional initiative's contention that the congregation is *the* fundamental form Christian witness must take in the public sphere today is not without its problems, as we will discuss in the next section; however, this emphasis helps counteract overly individualistic understandings of the Christian life. Christian faith is not a cerebral affair—a matter of privately cherishing a specific set of religious beliefs. It is a shared way of life, a way of being fully human in company with others, and a way of deeply engaging the world that God

24. Van Gelder and Zscheile, *Missional Church in Perspective*, 119.

so fiercely loves. We maintain relationship with the "other" we encounter within the Christian community, where tensions inevitably arise. In company with our siblings in faith, we also turn decisively outward, engaging the "other" in the most concrete and challenging sense. In Christ's name and with Christ's servant-like posture, we commit ourselves to support the well-being of the racially, ethnically, culturally, economically, and theologically different "other."

Limitations of Missional Interpretations of Christian Witness

The health of any theological conversation or movement depends on its capacity to be self-critical. While the missional initiative has energized and refocused many pastors and congregations for more credible public witness, even those deeply sympathetic to its aims have identified gaps, blind spots, or inconsistencies in missional thought and practice. In this section, we explore some of these problems.

An Idealized Portrait of the Congregation and Its Practices?

First, evidence shows that neither Christian practices nor the cultural formations we call congregations are as distinct from "the world" as we might imagine. In some expressions of missional thought, a missional view of the church is harnessed to a strong narrativist reading of Scripture—one that claims there is only one right way to "read" the story Scripture tells. This reading of Scripture can also lead to the assumption that the specific shape of Christian practices is derived, without remainder, from the story Scripture tells. In other words, Scripture tells a single, unequivocal story, and that story dictates a particular set of practices.[25] (Bryan Stone's work, discussed above, tends in this direction.) Such a wed-

25. I have discussed elsewhere and at more length why this is not the case with Christian practices. See Sally A. Brown, "Exploring the Text-Practice Interface: Acquiring the Virtue of Hermeneutical Modesty," *Theology Today* 66, no. 3 (October 2009): 279–94.

ding of missional theology, a strong-narrativist reading of Scripture, and a faithful-practices vision of the proper life of the church can lead to the insistence that the church is utterly distinctive from "the world" and that it is less than faithful unless it stands out as a social alternative and contrast culture over against an alien world. Yet one has to wonder where (and ultimately, whether) congregations capable of sustaining such radical differentiation from their culture exist, except in certain sectarian, separatist expressions of Christianity. (The Old Order Amish communities of Pennsylvania and parts of the American Midwest would be examples.)

Pastor and homiletician Patrick Johnson, while sympathetic to many of the emphases and aims of missional theology, questions whether we can speak quite so glibly about the distinctiveness of the Christian community and its practices. Johnson worries that "missional theologians do not take sufficient account of the sociocultural and religious complexity of congregations and the individuals in them." Inspiring as we may find the missional image of a highly cohesive church, steeped every week in a set of distinctive worship practices that translate into an unequivocal, coherent, and consistent redemptive public witness, Johnson questions its realism. He observes,

> The unspoken assumption seems to be that there is a relatively homogenous, coherent group called a "church" or "congregation," which can be set in distinction to a world that is "out there." Yet when you press more deeply, there is as much world "in here" as "out there." There is not a clear line between church and world, and there is a complex mixture in every individual Christian and congregation.[26]

As Johnson points out, congregations are made up of human individuals and families who have lives outside of the church. Those in our pews move rather fluidly among a great variety of sociocultural formations, each of these having its own norms and practices. Some of these overlap with the membership of a congregation; and while some of these communities of affiliation have values and aims that comport well with those of a person's Christian congregation, oth-

26. Johnson, *Mission of Preaching*, 228.

ers do not. They may, in fact, stand in direction competition with the congregation's values and goals.

Contemporary social theory argues similarly. As French ethnologist Pierre Bourdieu points out, practices (and this includes the practices of Christian communities) are inevitably hybrid constructions, shaped by the overlapping cultural formations that construct all social space.[27] They take their shape from multiple sources and cultural influences. These include the community's authorizing texts, but our practical orientation to our surroundings always reflects historical and contemporary influences, including many whose shaping influence is opaque to us. Without a doubt, the specific forms that Christian practices take in local congregational contexts can be *partly* accounted for by way of theological description—but only partly. No congregation's practices are "pure" embodiments of conscious theological convictions.

Theologian Kathryn Tanner likewise argues that the practices of any Christian congregation are inevitably "hybrids," reflecting in some ways that community's readings of Scripture, in others the "DNA" of the particular Christian tradition to which it is heir, and in still other ways, the habits and norms of the particular culture, or cultures, amid which it is embedded, and in which its members carry on their daily lives. As bracing as visions of the Christian congregation as an utterly distinct, Scripture-formed community may be (as argued, for example, in the proposals of Dietterich and Stone, discussed above), this idealized picture does not square with congregational life as we experience it in our society. Notably, even the practices of the earliest Christian congregations that we read about in the New Testament seem to show the influence of many overlapping sociocultural formations.

An adequately nuanced, more empirically informed picture of the life of a congregation would require that we describe it as evidencing considerable overlap with many other cultural formations in which its members have a stake. We need only to consider a couple of representative families or individuals in our own congrega-

27. Pierre Bourdieu, *The Logic of Practice* (Stanford, CA: Stanford University Press, 1990), 12–14, 39.

tions to recognize this dynamic. Church members have obligations to many cultural formations, each with its particular expectations and norms. These might include extended families (which have expectations around shared celebrations, caregiving, and problem-solving), cultural organizations, workplace cohorts, volunteer-service associations, like Meals on Wheels, political action groups, recreational or school-related cohorts, like a summer youth soccer league, and so on. Each of these cultural formations has its own authorizing "texts" and shared practices, and all of them overlap with, and bear upon, the hybridity of a Christian congregation's practices.

Clearly, some caution is in order, lest our theological ideals cause us to oversimplify our congregation's identity and witness, both in the pronouncements we make from the pulpit and the ministry strategies we plan. If preachers and other church leaders embrace an overly idealized notion of how the congregation should behave, one that fails to recognize the hybridity of the sociocultural forces that shape life in the pews, the result can be frustration for church members and leaders alike. When leaders claim an unrealistic formational exclusivity for the practices of the church, church members will labor under an unfair burden of guilt for the necessarily "hybrid" nature of their everyday lives.

Realism prompts us to recognize that Christian identity and witness in the world is a matter of constant negotiation. One does not leave one's "world" behind at the sanctuary door. Yes, living up to our baptismal vows shifts our priorities and nuances every affiliation in our lives; yet Christians inevitably—and legitimately!—have significant roles in, and obligations toward, many communities of affiliation other than the congregation. To be sure, we need to become as critically aware as possible of the (possibly compromising) pressures upon our lives of these other affiliations. Yet none of us can entirely escape these expectations and formational pressures. Despite the appeal of the "new monasticism" in some quarters, the fact remains that Christian communities are zones of complex sociocultural overlap among many different communities, not zones of "purely Christian" belonging and practice.[28]

28. For a brief introduction to the "new monasticism," see Jonathan Wilson-

Participants in the Spirit's Work:
Over Against or Alongside Others?

This brings us to a second, closely related concern: The implication that the public witness of the church depends on Christian communities becoming contrast cultures *over against* the world stands in considerable tension with a core tenet of missional thought. From its inception, missional thought has emphasized that the Spirit of God is at work not only in and through the church, *but in and through the world.*

In their 2011 retrospective analysis of missional scholarship and church practice, Craig Van Gelder and Dwight Zscheile point precisely to this tension in today's missional conversation. Its original, world-embracing pneumatology and understanding of the *missio Dei*—God's redemptive presence and activity—stands at odds with missional proposals that tend to focus on the church as the sole agent qualified to discern and participate in the redemptive work of God.

The movement of the Spirit in creation is embodied and public. It is not only the church but other communities of faith, as well, who seek to discover what God is doing in the world. A much wider horizon of God's movement in and through so-called secular space, people, and cultures is needed. The church does not have exclusive possession of God's presence and activity. All persons, made in God's image, are made to serve as cocreative creatures with God and in the world.[29] This is not to say that ecclesial communities, their distinctive practices, and their capacities for discerning the ongoing work of the Spirit in the world have no significance. It does mean that, if missional theologians and pastoral leaders are serious about their world-embracing pneumatological stance, then congregations should be eager to partner with others beyond the bounds of Christian fellowship whose commitments also align with the inclusive love and restorative justice of God, at work in the power of the Spirit in the wider world. In other words, our attitude

---

Hartgrove, *New Monasticism: What It Has to Say to Today's Church* (Grand Rapids: Brazos, 2008).

29. Van Gelder and Zscheile, *Missional Church in Perspective*, 113.

toward other faith communities needs to include discerning openness to the possibility that the Spirit will lead us into side-by-side
partnership with them, not "over-against" judgments or dismis-
siveness. Missional thought from its beginnings has been hospitable to the idea that other communities and individuals, whether of
other faiths or none, may also be committed to loving hospitality
toward strangers, justice for all, and the protection of society's most
vulnerable. And in these commitments, they contribute to God's
redemptive initiatives in the world.

Missional: Too White, Too Male, and Too Mainline?

As mentioned at the beginning of this chapter, the fact that, to date,
missional theology has been dominated by Protestant, "mainline,"
white male voices has limited its appeal for scholars and pastoral
leaders of color. Many scholars and leaders in congregations of color
agree, in principle, with the missional initiative's outward-turned
way of describing a congregation's vocation. Many also embrace
the insight that the Spirit is working redemptively, not only in and
through the church, but also beyond it, in and through the wider
world. A few have, in fact, adapted missional insights to their concerns and context.[30] Yet many pastors and theologians of color express concern that missional "insiders" have been slow either to
recognize or acknowledge the "whiteness" of naively universalized
claims about the church's failings.[31]

Critiques of the church that emerge from largely white, male,
"mainline" consultations cannot be generalized across all congre-

30. See, for example, David L. Everett, *Future Horizons for a Prophetic Tradition:
A Missiological, Hermeneutical, and Leadership Approach to Education and Black
Church Civic Engagement*, Missional Church, Public Theology, World Christianity
7 (Eugene, OR: Pickwick, 2017). A handful of dissertations by scholars of color—
African American, Asian, and Latinx—also engage missional insights for nonwhite
congregational settings.

31. For some of these insights, I am indebted to colleagues of color, including
Luke A. Powery, the dean of Duke University Chapel, and Kenyatta Gilbert, professor of homiletics at Howard University.

gations in twenty-first-century North America and Europe. When missional theologians speak in global terms of "the church," as if white, mainline failures were everyone's failures, and as if white, mainline Protestant scholars and pastors could speak, or even have the right to speak, to and about all congregations in all contexts, church leaders and theologians of color are rightly skeptical.[32]

Verge Network blogger Kyle Canty, a member of the black, mainstream church, is sympathetic to some of the missional movement's efforts to stake out a broader conception of Christian public witness in the world, yet he is concerned about what he sees as a lack of attention to issues of race implicit in its proposals. He writes,

> It is often said that Blacks need a seat at this "table" in order to influence what goes on as the movement becomes more mainstream. Why is it so hard to sit down at this table called the Missional Movement? Perhaps the answer lies in the fact that the missional movement is nestled inside of evangelicalism and this movement has not properly dealt with race.[33]

Canty further notes that the failure of the missional movement to attract the interest of a significant share of the leadership of historically black churches is owing, at least in part, to the fact that the movement's core problematic—the struggle of the "disestablished," mainly white, mainline Protestant churches to mount a credible public Christian witness in a religiously plural, globalized sociocultural landscape—operates with assumptions about the condition of the church that do not always reflect the specific challenges and concerns of black congregations, particularly urban congrega-

---

32. To own my own social location, I am a white female Presbyterian and an ordained minister of word and sacrament with eighteen years of parish and non-parish ministry experience in majority-white churches, before beginning to teach twenty-one years ago in seminaries with increasing ethnic and denominational diversity. These diversities have dramatically adjusted my view of church and world.

33. For a critical assessment of the missional initiative from an African American perspective, see Kyle Canty, "A Black Missional Critique of the Missional Movement," Verge Network, www.vergenetwork.org/2013/07/26 /a-black-missional-critique-of-the-missional-movement.

tions in the African American or Latinx worshiping traditions. For black, Latinx, Asian, and immigrant congregations, the experience of being a "contrast" community is hardly news, nor is the public responsibility of the churches to bear witness to God's love and justice within the communities they serve. Church leaders of color (and, I might add, students) are understandably skeptical when missional writers fail to own the limits of their social location and perspective, or to confess the complicity of their historic traditions in slave-holding or colonialist notions of mission.

Ironically (and sadly), missional thinkers have figuratively and literally walked right past hundreds of congregations of color from whom they could have learned much. Congregations of color have been deeply invested in the *missio Dei* beyond their sanctuary walls for decades, supporting with scant resources a costly witness for racial and economic justice before the world over generations.

As Christianity all over the globe becomes less white and less mainline, the missional initiative will need to broaden its scope. The future is likely to call for less prescribing and more listening. Like all primarily white theological initiatives, the missional initiative in both academy and church will need to recognize, confess, and address the sometimes naively white nature of its analyses and pre-scriptions, and welcome alternative accounts that scholars and pastors of color can supply concerning the crisis of Christian witness in twenty-first-century North America and beyond. Such openness will quite naturally loosen the tendency of missional thought to reflect mainline visions and values concerning congregational life and mission—since, while churches of color include many of the old mainline denominations, they include many others, as well.

Yet it may be the male-dominant character of missional thought that will be slowest to change. Without a doubt, women's voices have been in the mix, here and there, from the inception of the missional initiative two decades ago; but for this theological and ecclesial undertaking to remain truly relevant to twenty-first-century society, more of its work, scholarly and ecclesial, will need to be shaped by women. Women's insights into the nature of leadership and about the distinctive challenges of witness for justice that women face need to become more central. Moreover, the continuing struggle for women's empowerment as equals in church and society must be on the missional agenda, wherever Christians are serious about participating in the *missio Dei*, God's redemptive work in the world.

Missing from the Missional Map:
The Everyday Witness of Ordinary Christian Lives

We noted above that missional theologians emphasize communal, congregational practices as the primary form that Christian witness must take in the twenty-first century. As Patrick Johnson puts it in his theologically rich proposal for a more deeply missional approach to preaching, it is "axiomatic in missional conversations" that "the congregation is the basic unit of Christian witness."[34] As we noted earlier, missional theologians' emphasis on congregational practices as the primary form of Christian witness has provided an important corrective to excessive Western individualism.

Yet strikingly muted, so far, in the missional project is any discussion of Christian public witness in the twenty-first century *at the level of individual Christian believers acting in everyday, public space*. Without a doubt, when individual Christians succeed in bearing creative witness, in deed and word, to the inclusive love and restorative justice of God in their weekday world, their capacity to do so surely derives, in part, from the formational influences of congregations. We will have more to say about this interdependence between individual and community witness in chapter 4, where the task of foregrounding a congregation's shared Christian practices is the focus. Yet the missional significance of the witness of individual Christian lives in the ordinary settings and situations of daily life deserves far more attention than it has received to date.

Craig Van Gelder and Dwight Zscheile underscore this gap in the missional literature in their 2011 retrospective on developments in missional theology. While missional writers often contend that Christians are called to bear witness in the spheres of everyday life, note Van Gelder and Zscheile, the details of that

34. Johnson, *Mission of Preaching*, 104.

life of witness have so far been left vague. Noting "the significant gap many lay Christians perceive between what they experience at church and what they have to face in their daily lives," Van Gelder and Zscheile call for pastors and other congregational leaders "to take far more seriously the realities of the world in which Christians struggle to live faithfully each day." Pastors and preachers must help believers develop "daily discernment of God's movement in the 'secular' spaces in which they spend the great majority of their days."[35]

Van Gelder and Zscheile distill their concerns with a pointed question: "*How is it that ordinary Christians can authentically imagine and enter into participation in God's mission in their workplaces, homes, neighborhoods, and world?*"[36] They go on to suggest that if individual Christians are going to become active participants in the ongoing, redemptive work of God going on in the settings they experience day in and day out in the weekday world, pastors and lay leaders will need to transfer the process of theological discernment and agency to those in the pews:

> Leaders are responsible not for monopolizing theological discourse in the congregation but for *equipping people in the practice of theological imagination* for interpreting the Word and making sense of their *daily lives in the world*. It is the *people who primarily enact this work of interpretation and discernment* within a *Christian imagination for God's movement and presence* within and around them.[37]

My italics highlight three especially important features of this statement. First, what is at stake is "daily lives in the world." Most people's ordinary, everyday lives are undertaken in arenas of human action and interaction that are not constructed according to identifiably Christian aims or values. (We will have more to say in the next chapter about the social construction of the sorts of public

35. Van Gelder and Zscheile, *Missional Church in Perspective*, 154.
36. Van Gelder and Zscheile, *Missional Church in Perspective*, 153; italics added. The second of the three questions that guide this book is an adaptation of Van Gelder and Zscheile's way of framing this issue.
37. Van Gelder and Zscheile, *Missional Church in Perspective*, 156.

spaces where Christians and others take action and interact.) In many cases, a Christian believer is the only one in that setting who consciously identifies with Christian faith.

Second, the "work of interpretation and discernment" has to become the project of the people themselves, not something done by leaders (and preachers) with little understanding of the specific *fields of action* where congregation members spend most of their waking hours. Diverse, realistic sermon illustrations can help this process; yet what is ultimately at stake is developing in sermon listeners the imaginative capacities to move into their world and discern, in the challenging situations they face daily, opportunities to participate in the ongoing, world-transforming work of the Spirit.

Van Gelder and Zscheile's question underscores that Christians need more than advice from their preachers; they need the wisdom to exercise imagination rooted deep in the resources of Christian tradition, discernment to trace redemptive openings in ordinary situations, and the daring it takes to align themselves with God's radical mercy, restorative justice, and inclusive love in an unfolding scenario. In other words, one of the tasks of preaching today is to help those in the pew develop the sort of situation-specific, faith-driven tact that can be accessed not only in the calm, reflective safety of the Sunday morning, but also amid the press and turmoil of the places they work and socialize.

A third observation about Van Gelder and Zscheile's question is that they mention "imagination"—not once, but twice. Historically, Christian theology has treated imagination with a certain wariness; yet philosophers and lab researchers alike suggest that imagination is actually an essential element in the process of exercising agency (capacity to act) in any situation.[38] Imagination is precisely what we use to envision and test possible courses of action that may be off script—that is, outside the usual routines and expectations—in an everyday situation.

38. See, for example, Philipp Dorstewitz, "Imagination in Action," *Metaphilosophy* 47, no. 3 (2016): 385–405; and Mark Johnson, *Moral Imagination: The Implications of Cognitive Science for Ethics* (Chicago: University of Chicago Press, 1993).

A Challenge for Preachers:
Understanding the Everyday Field of Action

Van Gelder and Zscheile's concern about the everyday witness of individual lives lays down a challenge for pastors and preachers. If our job is to equip individual believers to discern and participate in the redemptive movement of the Spirit in the settings of their everyday lives, we need specific pulpit strategies that support this kind of imaginative, adaptive discernment. But we also need a better understanding of the dynamics of that *field of action* we call everyday life.

Most pastors and preachers have a grip on the field of action that is congregational life inside the sanctuary, in the fellowship hall, at the hospital or the soup kitchen, and even two thousand miles from home on a mission trip. But the fields of action where most Christians necessarily spend their everyday lives are dramatically different. First and foremost, the concrete fellowship of acting in concert and company with other believers toward a common goal is greatly suppressed, if not altogether absent, in the settings where most of those in the pews spend most of their waking hours. As we have already suggested, the average person's everyday life is made up of all sorts of hybrid zones in which the powerful, formative practices of multiple (and sometimes competing) sociocultural formations hold sway. Recent social theory implies that not all fields of human action are alike, and our range of agency (capacity for action) differs from one to the next. Our opportunities for action are affected by socially constructed differentials of power, official and unofficial; and any individual Christian may find himself or herself occupying a relatively powerful or relatively powerless position in a given setting or situation.

We will address these issues in the next chapter, but to help us think in more concrete, contextualized terms about these issues, I offer here a case study. It is based indirectly on the experience of a former parishioner, with names and details altered:

> Frieda, a woman in her mid-thirties, is a member of your church and chair of the community outreach committee. She attends worship

as often as she can and is eager to learn how Christian faith should shape her everyday life. After a painful divorce from an abusive partner, Frieda recently remarried. Her husband, Jack, doesn't share her Christian faith. Jack's family is mostly estranged from the church. Jack's own brother and sister-in-law cite the church's hypocrisy, as well as recent clergy abuse scandals. Besides, Jack works every other weekend at the local hospital and is glad Frieda feels comfortable going to church solo.

Recently, Frieda found herself at an out-of-town pool party, a family reunion for her new husband Jack's side of the family. It's an event held only once every five years. There are fifty or sixty guests, some relaxing in the folding lounge chairs they've brought and arranged near the pool, others chatting over the remains of lunch at tables around the yard. The host, Barry (a distant cousin of Jack's), has been helping himself to the beer keg regularly all day, as have others. A group of the beer imbibers are talking and laughing, trading off-color jokes with an occasional glance around to see that none of the kids at the party are nearby. Frieda is used to mixing with all kinds of people, so while she might not choose to party quite the same way, she's enjoying being with Jack and meeting more distant branches of his family.

But Frieda becomes concerned when the obviously drunk host grandstands for attention by forcing his eleven-year-old daughter Jennie to put on her aunt's amply built bathing suit and prance around the pool, beauty-queen fashion, for the crowd. The child says, "No," at first; but when her father Barry begins to raise his voice and suggests she's a "party pooper," Jennie complies. She is clearly uncomfortable parading for the crowd, her face red with embarrassment. Some of the guests are shaking their heads, commenting under their breath that Barry should know better, "but it's his party." Egged on by his buddies, who are howling with laughter now, Barry tells the girl to go around the pool a second time. There are more catcalls and whistles.

At this point, Frieda feels acutely uncomfortable with the abuse of generational and familial power she's witnessing. She shoots Jack a meaningful look, but he shrugs in a gesture of helplessness and shakes his head. Meanwhile, Jennie looks miserable. What can Frieda do? Should she create a scene? Walk up and confront their drunk host?

Grab Jennie and walk away with her? In so doing, Frieda could drive a wedge between her new husband Jack and his family. Frieda is a stranger here; she is a guest at this party. She really knows only Jack and (by name only) a couple of others who attended their wedding. Her leverage in this situation seems tenuous at best.

For many in our pews, Frieda's situation is not at all difficult to imagine. Her dilemma brings into view some of the social, cultural, and moral complexities that individual Christian believers encounter in ordinary situations every day, whether at the workplace, in a college classroom, at the exercise club, or in a weekend social situation. Amid ordinary situations like this one, Christians often feel compelled to take action, or speak up, out of Christian love and a concern for God's restorative justice; but how to do that—or whether it is even possible, given the constraints of a situation—isn't immediately clear. Frieda is dealing with at least three specific realities that bear upon her capacity to act in this field of action:

1. The situation represents the complex overlap of multiple sociocultural formations, or communities of shared interest. Frieda is experiencing multiple vectors of allegiance and obligation at the same time in this situation. Her different identities in varied communities of affiliation are resulting in a collision of different roles, values, and norms.

2. In a complex zone of overlapping cultural formations such as the one Frieda is experiencing, a Christian believer may not be in a power position. He or she may experience a considerable degree of constraint on his or her power to act (agency) in the situation at hand; and this relates to the competing roles, with their varying degrees of power, cited in #1.

3. Frieda finds herself in a situation where she is isolated from other Christian believers on whom she might rely for wisdom, support, or a shared intervention strategy. The missional ideal of Christian witness taking shape as a shared public practice undertaken by a Christian community does not help much here.

The vast majority of situations in which issues of justice and compassion are at stake present themselves to individual Christian believers on a small and local scale, as in this case. Frieda may have heard missionally inspired sermons about the need for her congregation to undertake communal social practices that bear public witness to God's redemptive intentions toward humanity and all creation. She may have heard a sermon about what justice means, or about how we should act on behalf of the vulnerable, not sit on the sidelines. In terms of the *values* that need to inform Frieda's "read" of her present situation, these sermons are helpful reference points. Perhaps missing, though, have been sermons that present models of inventive Christian faithfulness, at the individual level, adequate to the social complexities of real-world situations like this one. What might it look like to interrupt the *status quo* and interject action that testifies to a different vision of human dignity, amid all the constraints Frieda is experiencing?

First, Frieda must chart a course that takes into account four sets of competing expectations: (a) those of her new marriage to Jack; (b) those of the extended family (norms not necessarily identical with hers or even Jack's personal values); (c) the special, perhaps looser, norms of this specific time and place—a once-in-five-years, pull-out-all-the-stops party; and (d) those of the Christian community of which Frieda is an active part.

Second, a factor contributing to Frieda's dilemma is the sense of constraint she experiences in terms of her power to act (agency) in this situation. Overlapping communities of allegiance create complex vectors of power. At church, Frieda's role as chairperson of a significant committee gives her significant power. But in her marriage to Jack, her role and leverage for action in settings like this family reunion is uncertain; in fact, it is actively under negotiation. Those considerations aside, Frieda is a guest, not the host or a personal friend of the host. Practically a stranger here, Frieda occupies a relatively weak position in terms of questioning or disrupting these proceedings. Overplaying her hand (so to speak) could be costly, not only to herself but to Jack's relationship with the extended family, and costly, too, in terms of marital communication. Yet eleven-year-old Jennie's distress is real and immediate. Much is at stake.

Third, in the vast majority of the situations in which Christians must act, they do not find themselves in the company of other believers. Sermons that speak idealistically about the witness of the community are well and good; but rarely are Christian lives carried out in the bracing company of so much as a handful of Christian companions.

Frieda needs to hear sermons that recognize that she may very well have no fellow Christians to count on, in most of the ordinary settings of her life.

Frieda, and others like her, need to hear more sermons that characterize faithfulness as a matter of courageous, individual inventiveness in situations for which there is no clear map or playbook.

Next Steps

As we've shown, everyday situations rarely present obvious, unambiguous ways to manifest the mercy, love, and justice of God. In part II of this book, we'll begin discussing concrete preaching strategies that can help form believers for faith-inspired acts of courage in ordinary settings. But before we hasten toward the pulpit, we're well advised to take a page from the missional consultation and bring together with our theological and homiletical reflections some serious thinking about the dynamics of culture within which Christian witness takes place today. Some reflection on two preliminary questions, then, will occupy us in the next chapter. First, how do social theorists today describe the "social geography" of everyday situations like the one Frieda faces? And second, how can we best describe the kind of agile, yet faithful, action that complex situations like this one call for?

Further Reading:
Missional Thought and Missional Preaching

These publications represent a range of projects that coalesce around a missional view of the church, although not all are compatible in every respect with the argument of this book. Readers are encouraged to think critically not only about an author's explicit proposals, but also about the underlying assumptions about the scope and range of the *missio Dei*—God's work in the world—that informs them.

Barrett, Lois, et al. *Treasure in Clay Jars: Patterns in Missional Faithfulness.* Grand Rapids: Eerdmans, 2004.

Guder, Darrell L. *Called to Witness: Doing Missional Theology.* Grand Rapids: Eerdmans, 2015.

———, ed. *Missional Church: A Vision for the Sending of the Church in North America.* Grand Rapids: Eerdmans, 1998.

Johnson, Patrick W. T. *The Mission of Preaching: Equipping the Community for Faithful Witness.* Downers Grove, IL: InterVarsity Academic, 2015.

Leffel, Gregory P. *Faith Seeking Action: Mission, Social Movements, and the Church in Motion.* Lanham, MD: Scarecrow/Rowman & Littlefield, 2007. See especially chapters 8 and 9.

Tizon, Al. *Missional Preaching: Engage, Embrace, Transform.* Valley Forge, PA: Judson, 2012.

Van Gelder, Craig, and Dwight J. Zscheile. *The Missional Church in Perspective: Mapping Trends and Shaping the Conversation.* Grand Rapids: Baker Academic, 2011.

———. *Participating in God's Mission: A Theological Missiology for the Church in America.* Grand Rapids: Eerdmans, 2018.

Watkins, Eric Brian. *The Drama of Preaching: Participating with God in the History of Redemption.* Eugene, OR: Wipf & Stock, 2017.

CHAPTER 2

The Everyday Witness of Ordinary Christian
Lives as Faithful Improvisation

In part II of this book, we will explore ways that the sermons we preach can support Christians, individually, in their efforts to bear credible witness to their faith in the inclusive love, restorative justice, and radical mercy of the God we know through Jesus Christ. But before we can take up homiletical questions, we need to answer a prior one: What might such witness look like amid the complexities of everyday life in the twenty-first century?

We live in a time when societies around the globe wrestle with deep religious, cultural, racial/ethnic, class-based, and political tensions. In many places, this has translated into widespread, entrenched mistrust of the "other." A perceived scarcity of critical resources (territory, religious freedom, natural resources, jobs, or national security) quickly translates into the belief that some in the world pose a mortal threat to one's own safety and well-being. Fear burns bridges instead of building them; it builds walls instead of tearing them down. It feeds on stereotyping and toxic rhetoric. Strategic manipulation of social media can fan fear-driven belief systems into flames of political, ethnic, and religious fundamentalisms, which in turn can spawn extremist views and tactics.

I am indebted to Samuel Wells, vicar of St Martin-in-the-Fields, London, and visiting professor of ethics at Kings College, London, for the striking and apt phrase "faithful improvisation." I adapt it here to characterize the forms of action Christian individuals may undertake in the public spaces of everyday life to testify to the inclusive love, restorative justice, and healing mercy of God. See Samuel Wells, *Improvisation: The Drama of Christian Ethics* (Grand Rapids: Brazos, 2004), 66.

41

Christianity, like every religion, is vulnerable to being co-opted to ideological purposes. In a world of hate rhetoric and threats issued in God's name, a world in which many people live in social echo chambers and hear only voices just like their own, the question of what counts as credible witness to the God we have come to know through Jesus Christ is all the weightier. How might someone who believes that Jesus Christ is the firstborn of a new creation, evincing in his ministry and self-giving death the inclusive love, restorative justice, and radical mercy of God, bear witness to these convictions and the hope they inspire in ordinary situations? When polarizing rhetoric throws all who call themselves Christian into a single, extremist mold, the stakes are high.

Missional thought has done much to set a new framework and direction for Christian public witness. Christian communities, argue missional scholars, need to be outward-directed communities that practice inclusive love, healing mercy, and restorative justice in the world. They need to be concerned with the suffering world, not turned inward, preoccupied with their own maintenance.

Yet, as we discovered in the last chapter, one of the most important elements of Christian witness in today's world has been largely overlooked by most missional scholars: the witness of ordinary, individual Christian lives carried out in the everyday places where they work and learn, socialize and shop, volunteer and vote. If we are correct in our hunch that what goes on inside Christian congregations' sanctuaries is becoming less and less a matter of much public interest, it could well be the case that the credibility of Christianity's hope-driven vision for an inclusive human and cosmic future depends more than ever on the credibility of ordinary, individual Christian lives carried out in public spaces—workplaces of all kinds, schoolrooms and college classrooms, volunteer organizations and cultural clubs, fitness centers and athletic events.

In this chapter, I want to explore what such everyday, individual Christian witness, especially in increasingly multicultural and religiously diversified Western and westernized societies, might look like.

Craig Van Gelder and Dwight Zscheile, after assessing the missional movement's vision for the renewal of Christian communities, its achievements, and its challenges, leave us with this significant question about the nature of *individual* Christian witness: "*How is it that ordinary Christians can authentically imagine and enter into participation in God's mission in their workplaces, homes, neighborhoods, and world?*"[1]

Thanks to the social conditions in the world, noted a few paragraphs earlier, this question carries even more weight for us today than it did when its authors first posed it more than eight years ago. We need to frame our answers to this question with care. We run a double risk. First, we run the risk of oversimplifying the social complexity of the situations that our sermon listeners face every day of the week in the socially hybrid spaces where they work, learn, and raise their families. As Frieda's situation presented in the previous chapter suggests, even a fairly innocuous social situation, here at the cusp of the twenty-first century's third decade, can be fraught with tension. Families, workplaces, town meetings, and the like are likely to be crisscrossed by vectors of cultural and class difference having to do with understandings of family, gender, gender relations, and appropriate and inappropriate uses of power. Oversimplifying the dynamics of public situations as we explore what individual public Christian witness looks like will not help those in our pews.

We face a second risk: that we will be tempted to oversimplify what counts as Christian witness today. There was a time when "individual public Christian witness" meant, to many, confronting someone of another faith (or, on rare occasions, no faith) with "four spiritual laws" and asking him or her to "make a decision for Christ." Today, it is not hard to imagine that in many public situations, this approach could be considered, at the very least, offensive and, at worst, a form of abuse.

Van Gelder and Zscheile's question is a useful guiding question, not least of all because it contains some helpful theological clues. They speak of Christian witness in terms of *participation* and *imagination*. The broader theological scope of their work makes clear that,

---

1. Craig Van Gelder and Dwight J. Zscheile, *The Missional Church in Perspective: Mapping Trends and Shaping the Conversation* (Grand Rapids: Baker Academic, 2011), 153; italics added.

for them, the term *participation* points to an understanding—one that I share—that God is already redemptively at work in the world. We do not "take" God to a godless wilderness. God has preceded us; God invites our participation in the Spirit's work already underway. Our job is to discover the trajectory of that work and align ourselves with it.

The second term, *imagination*, implies that the shape that such participation needs to take cannot be read out of a rule book. Fitting Christian witness in any situation—especially public situations where multiple social realities, or cultural formations, overlap—requires modesty, tact, and creativity. We will be arguing later in this chapter that this creative work is not pure invention; it cannot be made up out of thin air. It has deep roots in the living and ever-adaptive traditions of Christian faith. But it does require of us imagination, inventiveness, courage, and a willingness to look foolish if necessary.

This chapter unfolds in three main sections. First, we'll explore contemporary social theory, in particular the work of social historian Michel de Certeau, to arrive at a more fine-grained understanding of how everyday life works, as a field of action. In order to construct a working model of Christian witness, we need to take account of the socially, culturally, and religiously hybrid nature of public spaces. We'll also have to pay attention to the differentials of power that structure social spaces and consider the way these differentials of social power confer different degrees of agency (power to act) on different players in that space. Agency is affected by one's official and unofficial roles in a space, as well as by gender and whether one is viewed as insider or "other" in the social microcosm of that space.

Our second quest in this chapter will be a more explicitly theological one. We will correlate the insights drawn from de Certeau with the work of two practical theologians, Charles L. Campbell (American) and Johann Cilliers (South African). Campbell and Cilliers, working with early Christian texts, including the New Testament, suggest that Christian witness works from a position of weakness, consonant with the weakness and folly of the cross. Such witness has a quality of redemptive "interruption" or subversion of reigning norms, calling into question the self-preserving, self-validating policies of established religious and political powers.

Finally, drawing on the work of theologians and ethicists in conversation with the practice of jazz improvisation, we will sketch a model for understanding the agile yet "grounded" creativity required of Christian believers who wish to bear credible witness to the inclusive love, restorative justice, and healing mercy of God in the settings and situations of everyday life.

Our explorations will take us to such far-flung zones of scholarly conversation as the rhetoric of folly and jest, theories of power and action in social space, theories about the role imagination plays in action, and the dynamics of jazz performance.

Understanding the Field of Action That Is Everyday Life

We begin by turning to the work of French social historian Michel de Certeau to gain a more nuanced sense of the play of power and agency in everyday fields of action, coupling that with a brief exploration of power and agency in the Gospels.

Michel de Certeau, Everyday Life, and the Tactics of the Weak

To describe the field of action that is everyday life requires a theory of action that helps us see how individual agents (producers of action) relate to the opportunities and constraints of their context. A model of social space that envisions discrete communities, each of them pursuing its own distinctive social practices, fails to take seriously the hybrid nature of nearly all public spaces. Consider the social dynamics that construct a workspace. Here certain players have the power to map that workspace's primary aims; others have assigned roles in carrying out those aims. Others enter the space with their own agendas; think, for example, of the medical-products salesperson visiting a local medical practice.

To help us understand these complex, hybrid zones of action in which some have more power than others, Michel de Certeau's theory of *the tactics of the weak* is a promising model.[2] De Certeau's work is complex and his language technical. A thorough assessment of his work on tactics as a specialized subset of human action would need to delve much more deeply and broadly into de Certeau's philosophical commitments. For present purposes, a brief mapping of his theory of tactical action can suffice.

De Certeau begins by positing that entities such as workplaces, religious institutions, or other social formations within a culture derive their basic structure from the agents in that situation who are the "powerful." Like other French social theorists, de Certeau is interested in the way that technocrats in a social system structure spaces to ends deemed appropriate by the powers that be. De Certeau uses the term *proper* to indicate spaces designated for particular purposes. A *strategy* is the goal-directed system, or rationale, that sets a space apart as a *proper* and determines which patterns of goal-directed action are appropriate to that proper, and which are not. Strategies are the *authorized* practices to be undertaken in that proper. Stretching de Certeau's model a bit, we might think of a courtroom, a prison, a fitness center, or even a church, as a proper in this sense, dedicated to specific uses and practices.

A *tactic*, on the other hand, is a repurposing of a proper space to ends other than the strategies set in place by those with the power to define and oversee what goes on in that space. The ones who repurpose, or subvert, the proper to use it for other aims and goals are the "weak"—those not in charge. A tactic is subtly subversive; it is "other" in a setting where conformity to sameness is expected. Tactical action "insinuates itself into the other's place, fragmentarily, without taking it over in its entirety [yet] without being able to keep it at a distance" (xix). Most everyday spaces, de Certeau argues, are contested spaces in which the weak pursue tactics, while the strong attempt to maintain the ordered strategies that serve their interests. Tactics, says de Certeau, are "clever tricks of the 'weak' within the order established by the 'strong,' an art of putting one

2. Michel de Certeau, *The Practice of Everyday Life* (Berkeley: University of California Press, 1984). In the paragraphs that follow, page numbers from this work will be given in parentheses in the text.

over on the adversary on his own turf, hunter's tricks, maneuverable, polymorphic mobilities, jubilant, poetic" (40).[3] The "weak," says de Certeau, exercise *agency*, causing the everyday "places" of their daily lives (which they can neither escape nor control) to function "in another register."

When de Certeau refers to the "weak," he does not have in mind weakness in terms of physical or intellectual capability; rather, this is his term for those agents in a space who do not possess strategic leverage over the mapping of that space, or proper. The "weak" may participate in the space voluntarily (for example, in order to gain employment or because they have agreed to attend an event), or they may find themselves in the space involuntarily (extreme examples would be a labor camp or prison). In either case, the space is mapped by assumptions and aims whose structure and expected behaviors the "weak" do not control, and which may not be to the advantage of the weak or comport with their values. De Certeau writes,

> The space of a tactic is the space of the other. Thus it must play on and with a terrain imposed on it and organized by the law of a foreign power. . . . It must vigilantly make use of the cracks that particular conjunctions open in the surveillance of the proprietary powers. It poaches in them. It creates surprises in them. It can be where it is least expected. It is a guileful ruse. In short, a tactic is an art of the weak. (37)

De Certeau cites instances of *tactical* action. For example, native peoples of South America under colonial rule appeared to assimilate the rituals, representations, and laws imposed on them by Spanish missionaries, yet subverted them, supplying the rituals and rubrics they were handed by the occupiers with other meanings—meanings that served their *own* purposes, not those of the oppressor. In another example, de Certeau describes a small drama

---

3. In this context, de Certeau also speaks of tactics as "warlike discoveries," accenting that tactics are a contestation on the part of the weak to pursue their own ends in the territory of the strong (32).

playing out on the floor of a furniture-making shop: a woodworker scavenges scraps to make a toy for one of his children, undetected by the owner of the shop (25). This subversion of the place and property of the business owner for the purposes of the worker is called *la perruque*. A more familiar example in the United States context plays out on the streets of every major city. When homeless street dwellers use recessed shop doorways as shelters and subway exhaust vents as heat sources, these are *tactics of the weak* playing out in landscapes constructed with other purposes in mind.

To act tactically is to be alert to time and timeliness, says de Certeau: "A tactic depends on time—it is always on the watch for opportunities that must be seized 'on the wing.' . . . It must constantly manipulate events in order to turn them into 'opportunities'" (xix). To put it another way, tactics are the timely insertion and assertion of the agency of the weak in the *spaces* that break open temporarily within the structured *place* that authorities define. Dense fog shrouds a contested border, and refugees who know the secret paths through the woods and fields sneak past the guards to safety. A city declares "vagrant-free" zones, and churches act tactically, invoking their status as tax-exempt entities, as well as citizens' freedom of religious affiliation, to provide accessible, safe gathering space.

The Tactics of the Weak as a Model for Everyday Christian Witness

De Certeau's theory of the *tactics of the weak* provides an intriguing model for reconceiving how Christians, even acting alone in settings and situations in which they have limited leverage, can take actions that testify to, and participate in, the dynamics of divine mercy and restorative justice. Might individual believers (like Frieda in the tense social situation described in chapter 1) train themselves to be alert to those "slippages" in a situation, seize their opportunities, and take action that promotes redemptive purposes?

Five features of de Certeau's theory of tactical behavior have intriguing resonances with the experience of Christian believers in the settings and situations they encounter in everyday life. First, "weakness" in relation to a particular situation is defined not in terms of some inherent physical or intellectual limitation, but in relation to the power structure that defines the strategic norms of a context. In the New Testament, Jesus—who is not inherently "weak"—aligns himself again and again with political and social weakness. The reign of God manifests itself as apparent weakness in relation to reigning powers, with the cross standing as the central emblem of this paradigm. In Frieda's situation, described in chapter 1, strategic power belongs to the host; and for many reasons, Frieda's power to influence the norms of the situation is weak, at best.

Second, tactics aim at ends and goals other than those of the dominant in a situation. The New Testament describes the ministry of Jesus and his followers as proceeding at cross-purposes with the norms and expectations of the reigning power structures, both the Jewish religious power structure and the powers of Rome. We find instances in the New Testament in which Jesus and his followers directly confront these powers and others in which they either elude or subvert the control of these dominant powers. More than once Jesus eludes would-be captors.

Third, the structured "places" presided over by the powerful are givens of everyday life for the weak; the nondominant do not have the choice to avoid (or, in de Certeau's terms, "keep at a distance") many of the situations in which they find themselves. Notably, Jesus does not suggest that his followers create a separate, parallel society. He and his disciples participate in the social structures of the culture, including synagogue worship, formal meals, religious festivals, and payment of taxes—although at times, Jesus adapts these spaces of shared activity so that they bear witness to the inbreaking reign of God.

Fourth, those who behave tactically do not "take over" a place or situation; rather, through abductive, co-optative action, they reappropriate a situation's dynamics, turning them to serve ends not necessarily envisioned or authorized by those in charge. (The resistance of Rosa Parks to a bus driver's order to relinquish her seat in the section designated for persons of color for the sake of a standing white passenger is an excellent example.)

Similarly, the ministry of Jesus is tactically subversive. Jesus does not take over or displace the power structures of the day; rather,

Jesus turns ready-to-hand situations to the purposes of the reign of God through moves of abduction—that is, by opportunistically co-opting situations to divine, redemptive aims. The cross, argues Duke scholar Dan Rhodes, is emblematic of this dynamic:

> The cross is a tactic that does not seek to end the reign of one political order by putting it to death so as to found the life of the next, but it sets out its operation within the social order by unraveling it internally, putting its internal identity of death to death, so as to free it for its use.[4]

Finally, the tactics of the weak are, if you will, *kairotic*; they depend on alertness to the "timeliness" of particular actions. Tactical alertness to time is a prominent marker in each of the Gospels, but particularly in the Gospel of John. Jesus's sense of the appropriate pursuit of God's reign, both for himself and those who follow him, unfolds according to an alertness to "the hour"—that is, to timeliness.[5]

Discipleship and the Tactics of the Weak in the New Testament

Although space does not permit a thorough exploration of the whole array of relevant New Testament texts that align tactics of the weak with Christian discipleship, several texts from the Corinthian correspondence and from Matthew's Gospel will serve to illustrate the alignment of discipleship with "weak" status and tactical action.

---

4. Dan Rhodes, "The Markings of Messianic Time: Repetition and Difference in Paul's Political Body," https://www.academia.edu/242418/Marks_of_Messianic_Time, 47. Of Paul's mode of action, Rhodes writes, "[Paul] engages whole heartily [*sic*] in the tactics of the weak, seeing this as the power of the Spirit unleashed with the resurrection of the Messiah to produce a particular kind of agency inside enemy lines" (45).

5. This point is emphasized by Rhodes, as well: "The power of the Spirit is nothing other than the power of the cross. . . . It is the power of the weak that, seizing hold of time instead of space, prevails against the strong by utilizing time" ("Markings of Messianic Time," 44).

The identification of Christian believers with all that the world considers weak is a persistent Corinthian theme. Notable are 1 Corinthians 1:26–31 ("God chose what is foolish in the world to shame the wise; God chose what is weak in the world to shame the strong"); 1 Corinthians 2:1–5 (the writer's self-identification, "I came to you in weakness and in fear and in much trembling"); 2 Corinthians 4:7–12 ("We have this treasure in clay jars . . . always carrying in the body the death of Jesus, so that the life of Jesus may also be made visible"); and 2 Corinthians 12:2–10 (the writer's report of his "thorn in the flesh" and the divine assurance, "My power is made perfect in weakness").[6] The power of God in the career of the apostles and church, as in the career and death of Jesus, is disregarded and dismissed as weakness by both religious establishment and state.

The identification of the presence and purposes of God with the socially, economically, religiously, and physically weak is a recurrent theme in Matthew, as well. The Beatitudes (Matt. 5:3–11) set up the theme of the "blessed weak" early in the gospel. The humble, not the proud; those who experience loss, not gain; those who hunger for righteousness instead of believing they have attained it; the persecuted, not the persecutors—these are the blessed.

Jesus's own ministry is characterized by abductive co-optation, or reframing, of situations structured by the religious authorities. Situations are made, in de Certeau's phrasing, to "function in a different register." In two Sabbath-day incidents in chapter 12—the disciples' unauthorized grain plucking and the healing of a man's withered hand in the synagogue—Jesus seizes opportunities to bypass the reigning propers of Sabbath and responds to these situations according to different rules, within the framework of God's reign of mercy. When interrogated about his authority in chapter 21, Jesus plays on the rules of legal debate, countering a question with another question, and stumping his interlocutors. Any answer they give about the origin of John's baptism, whether they deem it human or divine, bears consequences that will put their authority at risk. Challenged on the question of paying taxes to Caesar (Matt. 22:15–22), Jesus neither evades the question nor positions himself

---

6. All quotations are from the NRSV, unless otherwise noted.

against Rome directly. Instead, he reframes the debate according to his own understanding of ultimate value, which transcends local politics. The emperor's image-bearers (coins) are the emperor's; God's (human) image-bearers belong to none but God.

Intriguingly, Jesus is not the only one in Matthew to use the abductive logic and opportunistic tactics of the weak. When Jesus implies to a desperate Canaanite woman that she has no more entitlement to his attention than a dog, she is savvy; she turns the slight into a claim: dogs eat the crumbs from the master's table! Jesus, astonished, commends her faith (Matt. 15:21–28).

Christian Witness as Redemptive Interruption

De Certeau's theory of the tactics of the weak provides a thought-provoking lens for rethinking the witness of ordinary Christians in everyday settings in the contested sociocultural spaces that make up most Christians' everyday lives. To act tactically from a position of weakness will often require inventing a creative subversion of norms in spaces where the rules are not ours to define. This subversive dynamic in Christian witness has intriguing resonances with the work of two biblical interpreters and homileticians, cited earlier, Duke University homiletician Charles L. Campbell and practical theologian Johann Cilliers, who continues to pursue practical theological research in South Africa.[7]

Campbell and Cilliers argue that the gospel message is portrayed in the New Testament as a rhetoric of "folly." In a manner similar to Dan Rhodes, cited earlier, the point of departure for this rhetoric of "folly" is the cross. Citing one of the earliest known images of Jesus's crucifixion—a crucified figure with a donkey's head painted on the wall of what was once a boys' school—Campbell and Cilliers under-

---

7. Charles L. Campbell and Johann H. Cilliers, *Preaching Fools: The Gospel as a Rhetoric of Folly* (Waco, TX: Baylor University Press, 2012). In the paragraphs that follow, page references to this work are given in parentheses in the text. I have bracketed the term *redemptive* below, since it is not used explicitly in the text but seems to me implicit in Campbell and Cilliers's theological understanding of human agency shaped by the cross.

score the widespread opinion in the early days of the church that the notion of a "god" being pinned to the cross was purely and simply absurd, since the cross represented the ultimate loss of dignity and power (2–6). Crucifixion was designed, in fact, to be a cruel public farce, humiliating its victims and rendering them utterly impotent in the face of the power of the Roman state. The very fact that Jesus became the victim of such a death marked him as one more impotent fool who had dared to oppose the divine authority of Caesar and the juggernaut of the Roman army.

Yet, theologically, the cross proves to be the inbreaking of God that defeats the ultimate power wielded by the powers that be—the power of death. The cross is the disarming of all powers that retain their authority by threat and deadly violence. The "weak" power of God cuts across the grain of the domination-subordination axis with a wholly different potency that absorbs violence and defeats death by undergoing it. God vindicates Jesus's fidelity-unto-death to this alternative matrix of power by the raising of Jesus as the Christ, Lord of a new creation, on the third day. Our lives begin anew at the foot of the "foolish" cross. There we are freed from enslavement to this world's systems of power, let in on the deep secret that the powers of this world have not guessed: the "weakness" and "foolishness" of the cross is God's reality-transforming, irreversible destabilization of the systems of this world.

The "foolishness" of the cross stands in continuity with Jesus's lived interpretation of the reign of God. Throughout his ministry, we find Jesus unmasking the foolishness of self-obsessed, self-aggrandizing power, whether exercised by Rome or by the "righteous" leaders of synagogue and temple (103–26). In Luke 13, Jesus heals a severely bent-over woman. When the synagogue leader raises a loud objection, Jesus exposes the heartlessness and hypocrisy of the interpretation of Jewish religion he represents—one that allows beasts of burden to be led to water on a Sabbath but, in the name of forbidding Sabbath "work," would leave a woman bent and bound by pain.

Campbell and Cilliers also cite teachings of Jesus that commend jester-like, hyperbolic action to unmask the pretentious power of Rome. A prime example is Jesus's teaching that his followers should carry the gear of a Roman soldier not just one mile (the distance of portage for which soldiers could, by law, conscript a Jewish person), but to carry the gear also a second mile. Jesus knew, of course, that thanks to a tendency of soldiers to abuse this privilege, they were strictly forbidden to force a person to go a second mile. Thus, a disciple's service in the name of the "foolish," anointed one would leave a discomfited soldier looking like a foolish lawbreaker himself.

In addition, certain of Jesus's actions in Holy Week constitute game-changing, redemptive "interruptions" of expectations. Jesus's triumphal entry into Jerusalem looks anything but triumphant. He arrives not through the west gate, which symbolized conquering power, but through the east gate, symbolizing peace. He chooses to ride in *not* on a steed, symbolizing military might, but on the very symbol of foolishness, a donkey. This jest-like, hyperbolic performance of humility is timed to coincide with the ostentatious annual arrival of the imperial cohort and thus functions as a parody of status quo power, through and through (23–26).

After his arrest, Jesus "foolishly" stands mute before his interrogators and, ultimately, "foolishly" refuses to free himself from the cross, despite mockery. "He saved others, but he cannot save himself," cry the passersby. "If he is the King of Israel, let him come down now from the cross, and we will believe in him!" (see Matt. 27:42).

The gospel's way in the world, argue Campbell and Cilliers, is portrayed again and again in the New Testament as (1) a way of weakness in the face of self-confident, dominating systems, (2) agility in the liminal margins of such systems, and (3) "jesting" that destabilizes the "closed seriousness" of regimes designed to control, to dominate, and to intimidate (79, 102, 166). Thus, Campbell and Cilliers urge preachers to adopt a risky "rhetoric of folly"—a rhetoric characterized by reversal, hyperbole, and unmasking—that correlates with the destabilizing "foolishness" of the cross. Preachers become "agents of [redemptive] interruption" when they question or unmask the fear that lurks behind the swaggering threats of the powers of this world. Further, preachers are tellers of counter-stories—narratives that foreground the fragmentary evidences all around us of God's present redemptive action. Preaching aligned with the weakness of the cross may also include privileging the face and perspective of whoever in one's context may count as "other" for the congregation, reframing present realities in the horizon of God's promised newness, and using metaphor to reveal liminal spaces of dynamic transformation (162–80).

Campbell and Cilliers focus primarily on preachers themselves as "agents of interruption." Yet their work suggests that the everyday witness of ordinary Christians in the settings where they work and socialize, volunteer and vote, can also be thought of as undertaking subversive acts of *redemptive interruption*. Might Christian witness for Frieda mean interrupting the scene of Jennie's humiliation with a "foolish" scene of her own? Might one of our preaching tasks be to help listeners cultivate a sense of gospel-inspired, playful, "otherwise" agency that interrupts the regimes and routines of thoughtless or oppressive abuses of power?

Christian Witness as Faithful Improvisation

We opened this book by calling to mind four singular individuals—Rosa Parks, Vedran Smailovic, the Tiananmen "Tank Man," and Malala Yousafzai—who acted with vision, courage, and creativity to interrupt the reigning assumptions and purposes of the dominating powers in fraught situations. In each case, whether directly or indirectly, their daring acts broke open space for "interruptive" acts on the part of others, creating a ripple effect that destabilized fixed systems of oppression.

Of these four, only Rosa Parks has explicitly connected the action she took with Christian faith.[8] Yet all of these unforgettable actions strike me as important clues as we seek to understand the potential of individual Christians to align themselves with the mercy, love, and justice of God in the world, bearing witness to these realities in the ordinary settings of their lives. These individuals' stories inspire us to imagine that all of us—women and men, young and old—can participate in the ongoing, redemptive work of God in everyday

8. Rosa Parks with Gregory J. Reed, *Quiet Strength: The Faith, the Hope, and the Heart of a Woman Who Changed a Nation* (Grand Rapids: Zondervan, 1994), 54–55.

spaces like city buses, public squares, residential neighborhoods filled with tension and mistrust, and classrooms. The memorable actions of Rosa, the "Tank Man," Vedran, and Malala exemplify the "agency of [redemptive] interruption" to which Campbell and Cilliers point.

The strategic, power-shifting acts of redemptive interruption undertaken by these memorable figures is not the sort of thing one learns from any rule book. Each of these persons drew on commitments and visions deeply woven into their sense of themselves. Each of them drew on patterns of practice that were already part of the repertoire of their lives. These deep commitments, guiding visions, and familiar practices became the resources on which they drew in a critical moment that demanded a courageous act of redemptive interruption. In other words, their actions—their discerning departures from habit and routine—depended on the ability to draw on deep wells of conviction and know-how, and they put their knowledge to use in a creative way adapted to a critical moment and circumstance.

Another way to think of this type of action is in the framework of improvisational performance. Improvisation—particularly improvisational jazz performance—is not spun out of fantasy; it draws on a deep tradition with both diachronic and synchronic dimensions. It stretches back in time through generations of artistry. At the same time, this living tradition is being extended in diverse settings, where it is reshaped by an array of different circumstances and enriched by diverse musical cultures. This art of deeply traditioned innovation is a useful model for thinking about the dynamics of Christian witness in ordinary settings and situations.

Jazz Improvisation and Christian Witness: Traditioned Innovation

Significantly, classic jazz improvisation is not made up out of nothing; rather, it is rooted in a deep tradition of component skills, practices, performances, and paradigms. Responding to the demands of a particular time, place, and ensemble, a jazz improvisationist draws on deep wells of tradition and skill to create something apt to the moment and situation.

To play jazz competently, a musician spends hours a day over years immersed in mastering the practices and imitating the improvisational know-how of a vast company of other jazz musicians, contemporary and also historical. This indwelling of the musical tradition of jazz includes not only learning by heart a vast number of melodies that have furnished the imaginations of dozens of jazz artists of the past, but also learning by heart classic chord progressions and riffs (melodic variations based on those chord changes). As we explore the dynamics of jazz improvisation, we will begin to detect analogies to the way that Christians may develop instincts for taking creative, contextually fitting action in a situation that bears witness to the redemptive presence and activity of God.

Sam Wells, vicar of St Martin-in-the-Fields and former dean of Duke University Chapel, reminds us that improvisation is not "spontaneous anarchic autonomy."[9] Improvisation, whether we are considering dramatic performance (as Wells primarily does) or musical performance, works within guiding principles. Second, improvisation as a mode of creative action is not, as Wells puts it, "demonic." Improvisation is not a corruption of art or an attack upon tradition, nor is it facetious or trivial. Rather, the art of improvisation builds, both in theater and in music, out of the wisdom of past performance to create fresh performative possibilities in response to new contexts.[10]

Theologian Ann Pederson appropriates jazz improvisation as a heuristic model for understanding the nature of human and divine creative activity, and their interaction, in a process-theology framework.[11] In jazz, notes Pederson, the basic materials on which a jazz soloist or ensemble draws are the structure of the basic melody and chord changes of an established tune—often, in traditional jazz, a tune regarded as a classic in the jazz world. The ensemble

---

9. Wells, *Improvisation*, 17.

10. Wells, *Improvisation*, 66–69.

11. Ann Pederson, *God, Creation, and All That Jazz: A Process of Composition and Improvisation* (St. Louis: Chalice, 2001), 34.

plays upon this structure, bringing to the moment of creation the particular musical traditions represented in the ensemble. A performance may also function as musical "commentary," of sorts, on the larger sociocultural context surrounding the time and place of performance.

Citing Mary Catherine Bateson's work with the jazz analogy in her work *Composing a Life*, Pederson stresses that any improvisational art form combines familiar elements with novel ones. Such performance follows an underlying "grammar" and yet explores its latent possibilities in new ways. Pederson writes, "Jazz exemplifies a kind of creativity that holds together the individual and community, freedom and constraint, structure and chance. Improvisation helps us deal with the ambiguities life presents because it helps us confront the unfamiliar with the familiar, the chaotic with order."[12]

As Wells emphasizes, improvisation is an artfulness deeply rooted in a tradition. Jazz musicians make reference to this *traditioned* character of jazz in three respects. First, behind every classic jazz performance lies a widely recognized repertoire of tunes, known to both jazz performers and experienced listeners alike. Second, alongside this traditional reservoir of melodies and chord structures, there exists a second layer of tradition in the form of well-known improvisations laid down by greats of the past— performances either passed down from artist to artist or captured in recordings. Such honored improvisational performances are sometimes musically reiterated in homage to the musicians on whose shoulders each new generation of improvisationists stands. Every artful improvisationist is the embodiment not only of innovation at the forefront of a tradition's development, but also the keeper of the tradition's past. Yet that past is not kept to be enshrined, but to be the inspiration for new, previously undreamed possibilities of performance. This is the essence of any living tradition: it can survive only by growing and adapting in response to the demands of new challenges.

Preacher and jazz pianist William G. Carter elaborates on the "traditioning" element in jazz as he reflects on his own process of

---

12. Pederson, *God, Creation, and All That Jazz*, 34.

learning to play jazz.[13] Carter recounts how his teacher insisted that there was simply no substitute for studying the work of jazz musicians he admired, laboriously transcribing their work, and then mastering it with his own fingers.

Musicians become capable of creatively extending the jazz tradition by immersing themselves in it and mastering others' ways of building on that tradition. Carter stresses that this includes not only the core melodies and chord progressions that comprise one's musical "palette," but the unique ways that musicians of the past have mined that tradition and built upon it. Carter comments, "When jazz musicians improvise, sometimes they 'quote' another musician's material as a way of negotiating unfamiliar ground."[14]

One learns, in other words, to extend the jazz tradition in one's own time and cultural setting both by listening to those who have done so with exceptional ability and by physically imitating those masterful innovations of the past. As one masters the improvisational achievements of forebears in the art, one becomes fluent in providing one's own "commentary" on the tradition, bringing to a particular melody and chord structure the *otherness* of the present moment and one's particular musical sensibility.

The Everyday Witness of Ordinary Christian Lives as Faithful Improvisation

Jazz improvisation proves to be an illuminating model for reimagining the dynamics of Christians' everyday, public witness. Ann Pederson suggests three specific gains when we reimagine Christian life and witness through the lens of improvisation. First, this view of Christian faith and witness alters our perception of the *otherness* of settings, persons, or sociocultural constructions we encounter. Instead of being perceived as threats, these manifestations of otherness become invitations to discover fresh interpretations of the tra-

13. William G. Carter, "On Speaking What We Hear," *Journal for Preachers* 14, no. 1 (1990): 25–35.
14. Carter, "On Speaking What We Hear," 4.

dition to which we are heirs.[15] Second, the improvisational model as a lens for creative action takes seriously the fluidity and complexity of lived settings and situations, as well as the fluidity of our individual and collective responses to them. No two artists' improvisational interpretation of a tune in a given setting will be the same.[16] Third, the lens of improvisation keeps our theological traditions essential yet open ended. Our authorizing texts and long-standing practices become resources for creativity, rather than a stifling, ironclad fortress built of rules, directives, and prohibitions.[17]

In other words, Christian faith is a living tradition that believers inhabit and extend. Both its stories and its core practices fund the improvisational "performances" of God's liberating mercy, inclusive love, and restorative justice in ever-new situations. We cannot assume that quoting John 3:16, the Ten Commandments, or something from the Sermon on the Mount will be sufficient to the complex settings and situations of twenty-first-century life. On the other hand, these materials are not irrelevant; they are part of the reservoir of deep wisdom that fuels faithful, yet innovative, improvisational witness to the redemptive work of God in our world. Embodying in act and word the contours of God's promised future amid the settings of everyday life becomes far more than repeating, move for move or note by note, a fixed script or score; rather, responding to the flux of everyday situations in terms of God's promised future draws out of us the disciplined daring of improvisation.

A primary task for preachers, then, will be to help our listeners develop a deep "repertoire" on which to draw. In order for them to undertake improvisational, redemptive interruptions of the status quo that are living extensions and adaptations of the deep Christian tradition of witness that precedes them, members of our congregations need to learn the resources of Scripture and tradition. The point is not to simply repeat and replicate (although at times, that in

15. Pederson, *God, Creation, and All That Jazz*, 62. Pederson's term is *unfamiliar*; I prefer *otherness*, which evokes more of the "not-same" challenge of difference.

16. Pederson, *God, Creation, and All That Jazz*, 64.

17. Pederson, *God, Creation, and All That Jazz*, 76.

itself may count as tactical wisdom); rather, the point is to tap into the Christian present and past so as to respond creatively within present-day settings and situations that our forebears in faith, biblical and otherwise, could not have foreseen.

The resources of Christian tradition include not only the canonical Scriptures, but also historic creeds and confessions. These documents are themselves creative interpretations of the tradition in response to the crises and demands of past moments in history. In addition, Christian tradition includes a web of practices, particularly the core practices of Christian worship. These practices function both as a formative matrix that orients us to the horizon of God's future and, at the same time, a repertoire of paradigmatic performances of God's mercy, love, and justice. We will focus particularly on preaching that explores and illuminates Christian practices, in chapter 4.

Improvisation and the Significance of Formational Communities

We conclude this chapter with a clearer picture of the social landscape of everyday life and a model of individual Christian witness in everyday life that combines a deep rootedness in Christian faith and practice with the element of improvisational creativity. This model of Christian witness suggests that Christians who bear creative witness to God's redemptive work in the world—who become agents of tactical, redemptive interruption—are not born; rather, they are formed. The kinds of communities that missional scholars envision play a critically important role, then, in shaping individual believers for inventive, daring witness.

Rosa Parks, Verdan Smailovic, and others became creative agents of redemptive interruption, at least in part, because of the communities of knowledge and practice that shaped them. They had been formed by communities that, in different ways, nourished in them the vision, skill, and imagination to act when the moment for action presented itself. As activist and author Rick Chamberlin writes of Rosa Parks,

> Perhaps the most damaging myth about Rosa is that she acted alone.
> In fact, she worked for years with other social justice and civil rights
> activists. . . . She served as secretary for and was a member of her local
> NAACP chapter [and] attended workshops . . . to study racial deseg-
> regation tactics and Gandhian resistance methods. . . . Her decision
> to refuse to move to the back of the bus so that a white rider could
> have her seat was made in the context of a community.[18]

Warning against a peculiarly American tendency to valorize the
maverick, as if "our heroes act alone and appear on the scene
as if dropped from heaven," Chamberlin urges us "to remember
[Martin Luther] King [Jr.] and others like him as ordinary human beings who did extraordinary things with the help of other
ordinary people."

For Parks, Smailovic, the unidentified "Tank Man," and Malala
Yousafzai, there came that critical juncture of place and opportunity
in which they had to act—to do what they could, drawing upon
an alternative interpretation of the world that inspired innovative
action. In critical moments, each of these individuals chose to in-
voke an alternative vision of human flourishing in defiance of the
ironclad ideological structures of segregationist doctrine, genocidal
hate, brute force in the name of national stability, and misogynist
totalitarianism. The alternative vision that inspired each of them
did not come out of nowhere; it had been nurtured in them by a
community. In the last analysis, Chamberlin concludes, "the power
of one rests in numbers."

In an important sense, then, missional theologians are right to
claim that the congregation's communal, public witness is "logically
prior" to that of individuals.[19] The worship action we call preaching
is *itself* a communal practice, part of a complex web of practices
that have the potential to form within us deep wisdom and habits

18. Rick Chamberlin, "Let Us Honor Rosa Parks—By Shattering the Myths
about Her," http://www.commondreams.org/views/2005/10/30/let-us-honor-rosa
-parks-shattering-myths-about-her. The quotations in the paragraphs that follow
are also from this source.

19. Patrick W. T. Johnson, *The Mission of Preaching: Equipping the Community
for Faithful Witness* (Downers Grove, IL: InterVarsity Academic, 2015), 197.

Everyday Witness as Faithful Improvisation

of action that enable us to act with tactical, innovative faithfulness amid the challenges of our Monday-to-Saturday world.

Foregrounding the Improvisational Tactics of the "Weak": Two Sermons

All too often, preachers who want to encourage courageous public witness in their listeners do that by running down a tattered list of standard motifs: "We must care for the unloved. We ought to be the ones speaking out for the oppressed and visiting the lonely. If we believe what we say we do, we ought to be giving more of our time, talent, and treasure for the needs of others. Invite a neighbor to church. Tell someone what Jesus has done for you." There is nothing wrong, really, with any of this; but much of it trades on guilt as its chief tool of motivation, none of it is very specific, and—worst of all—none of it is news. Listeners to sermons that end this way leave church with a longer to-do list than they came in with, and have endured a scolding, to boot.

Inspiring faithfully imaginative, improvisational action calls for something else. Preachers do well to spend less time tacking to-do lists on the end of their sermons, and more time undertaking in the pulpit vivid, realistic acts of imagination that portray faith-driven, risk-taking, improvisational action that shifts the balance of power toward grace and hope. The two sermons discussed here do just that.

The first, Baptist preacher Nancy Hastings Sehested's sermon "Let Pharaoh Go!," takes up the story of the two midwives who defied Pharaoh (Exod. 1:8–22), interweaving it with the political situation in the United States at the time it was preached. Thomas G. Long's "Country Songs and Easter Hymns," based on Luke 24:36–49, tells a contemporary story in which tactical, grace-filled action interrupts a tension-filled situation one spring afternoon at a baseball stadium.[20]

20. Nancy Hastings Sehested, "Let Pharaoh Go!," in *And Blessed Is She: Sermons by Women*, ed. David Albert Farmer and Edwina Hunter (San Francisco: Harper & Row, 1986), 211–19; and Thomas G. Long, "Country Songs and Easter Hymns,"

63

| Nancy Hastings Sehested, "Let Pharaoh Go!"

Sehested's sermon was preached in the 1980s, during the Reagan era, in which social programs benefiting the country's most vulnerable citizens were being systematically cut back to lower taxes and stimulate economic growth. Her sermon is "coded" to address these realities.

Sehested sets the scene by evoking the bone-rattling terror of the pharaoh who sees the Hebrew slaves multiplying like rats. She tells us how the fear-driven monarch summons Shiphrah and Puah, two Hebrew midwives, and "explains" that, "for the good of the nation and for the security of the children of Egypt," he is making them his allies in "a secret and daring mission" to eliminate the boy Hebrew babies. They must kill all male Hebrew babies as they are born (Exod. 1:15–16). Sehested observes,

> Pharaoh had no idea what he was asking. All he could see was his precious and imagined threat to Egyptian national security. All he could see were two ordinary women who had no power, whom he considered weak, and who would certainly obey him. But Shiphrah and Puah knew who they were. . . . They knew they had no power before Pharaoh, so they let Pharaoh go—to think his own thoughts—to go his own way—while they followed their way assisting in life.[21]

The midwives defy the pharaoh's order consistently, their undeterred dedication to birthing life contrasted skillfully by Sehested with the maniacal terror of the pharaoh.

Deftly summoning the current political situation onto the stage, Sehested creates a litany through the middle section of the sermon, asking again and again, "Who are our pharaohs?" Our pharaohs are those powers that convince us that our situation is either too complex, too entrenched, or too dangerous. Pharaoh is whoever or whatever has us persuaded that we are too weak to act effectively.

---

in *Whispering the Lyrics: Sermons for Lent and Easter, Cycle A, Gospel Texts* (Lima, OH: CSS, 1995), 129–36.

21. Sehested, "Let Pharaoh Go!," 214.

Sehested bids us push, like the midwives, through the doors of the "birthing rooms" of justice and compassion, despite the powerful who forbid or dismiss our work, for "we are the people who follow the life-bearing God . . . the weak who confound the strong."[22]

Sehested's sermon unequivocally names, encourages, and celebrates the daring, improvisational tactics of the weak, motivated by the love and justice of God, in territory where our power seems limited.

| THOMAS G. LONG, "COUNTRY SONGS AND EASTER HYMNS"

Tom Long's "Country Songs and Easter Hymns" actually employs *both* the strategy of metaphorical renaming of space *and* foregrounding the unlikely agency of the weak. In this sermon, which asks us to reenvision the city, in all its frank secularity, as the arena of divine redemptive action, Long takes us to a baseball stadium where a drama plays out. As a foul ball arcs toward the wobbly, baseball-gloved hand of a little boy who clearly has more aspiration than experience going for him in the realm of baseball skill, a nattily dressed guy whose attitude says he feels entitled to baseballs and most everything else shoves the kid and snatches the ball out of the air. Onlookers, immediately enraged, set up a chant: "Give the kid the ball!" The ball-swiper is unmoved. Then someone down the row gets up and, instead of shouting, talks calmly to the man. No one knows what was said, but the ball is handed over, and applause breaks out all around the stadium. More remarkably, the next foul ball that's caught is silently handed over to the fellow who relinquished his ill-gotten catch, and others are caught and given away. The timely intervention of an anonymous person, calm enough to simply talk and courageous enough to try it, creates the opening for unexpected goodness. The crowd "had come that night to see a baseball game, but witnessed instead a city parable of justice and grace."[23]

---

22. Sehested, "Let Pharaoh Go!," 217. Note Sehested's metaphorical reframing of the critical space that calls for our decisive public action as "the birthing room," aligning our potential actions with the daring of the midwives.

23. Long, "Country Songs and Easter Hymns," 133–34.

In addition to foregrounding the subtle, but crucial, agency of an unremarkable baseball fan in this sermon, Long also develops the city itself as a metaphor for *all* places where the church finds itself—places of "wild diversity" and cultural richness, deep trouble and grace-filled, serendipitous possibility. There the church, when it is alert, can experience not self-absorbed fear, but the redemptive power of God.

Sermons such as these do not scold or prescribe. They awaken imagination to the way that the gospel-animated tactics of the weak work in the interstices of time and place to welcome the purposes of God. They challenge us to risk creative, subversive, grace-infused action in tension-filled situations, choosing to see those situations as arenas of redemptive possibility. These preachers fuel our hope that individual Christians may become "agents of [redemptive] interruption" amid the ordinary scenes and situations of their lives—even, or maybe especially, in settings where they appear powerless.

The four chapters in part II of this book explore four specific preaching strategies that, used consistently by a preacher over time, can support the imaginative, improvisational testimony of Christians to the reign of God in the everyday places where ordinary, individual Christian believers experience their Monday-to-Saturday lives.

Further Reading:
Improvisation and Imagination in Theology and Action

Some of the works listed here focus on varied approaches to the role of imagination in theology and preaching. Others take up improvisation as a heuristic model for envisioning theologically inventive discourse, including inventive action.

Bryant, David J. *Faith and the Play of Imagination: On the Role of Imagination in Religion.* Macon, GA: Mercer University Press, 1989.

Green, Garrett. *Imagining God: Theology and the Religious Imagination*. Grand Rapids: Eerdmans, 1998.

———. *Theology, Hermeneutics, and Imagination: The Crisis of Interpretation at the End of Modernity*. New York: Cambridge University Press, 2000.

Johnson, Mark. *Moral Imagination: The Implications of Cognitive Science for Moral Reasoning*. Chicago: University of Chicago Press, 1993.

Kelsey, David H. *Imagining Redemption*. Louisville: Westminster John Knox, 2005.

Norgaard, Martin. "Descriptions of Improvisational Thinking by Artist-Level Jazz Musicians." *Journal of Research in Music Education* 59, no. 2 (2011): 109–27.

Pederson, Ann. *God, Creation, and All That Jazz: A Process of Composition and Improvisation*. St. Louis: Chalice, 2001.

Thomas, Frank W. *How to Preach a Dangerous Sermon: Preaching and Moral Imagination*. Nashville: Abingdon, 2018.

Wells, Samuel. *Improvisation: The Drama of Ethics*. Grand Rapids: Brazos, 2004.

PART II

Preaching to Shape the Everyday Witness of Ordinary Lives

CHAPTER 3

Promise-Grounded Hope: Reading Word and World through the Lens of Divine Promise

Lived faith in the everyday world, says practical theologian Craig R. Dykstra, is "appropriate and intentional participation in the redemptive activity of God."[1] Dykstra's definition suggests that a first task for preachers who want to support such "appropriate and intentional participation" is to help our listeners *see* what is not obvious: the work of the Spirit percolating through the fissures and opportune moments of business as usual in ordinary situations. Guiding this chapter, then, is a homiletical question: *How can our preaching equip those in the pews with the "depth" vision they will need to discern pathways of redemptive action in ordinary, everyday situations?*

Prerequisite to a new way of acting is a new way of seeing. This chapter, then, is about helping our listeners see ordinary situations differently, in the extraordinary light of divine promise. The kind of vision that's needed is not some sort of paranormal insight, but something more straightforward: the capacity to "see double" or, to quote James F. Kay, to see "stereoscopically."[2] In other words, preachers need to help their listeners perceive ordinary situations in two ways: first, with stark and unflinching realism about both life-enhancing and life-denying dynamics present in situations; and

---

1. Craig R. Dykstra, "What Is Faith? An Experiment in the Hypothetical Mode," in *Faith Development and Fowler*, ed. Craig R. Dykstra and Sharon Parks (Birmingham, AL: Religious Education Press, 1986), 55.

2. James F. Kay, "The Word of the Cross at the Turn of the Ages," *Interpretation* 53, no. 1 (1999): 51.

second, in light of the promises of God, kept and being kept in Jesus Christ, to make all things new.

To see any situation in light of divine promise is to see it not as it presently is, but to reimagine it as it *could* and *should* be—as it *will* be—when, in the power of the Spirit, the dynamics of inclusive divine love, restorative justice, and healing mercy have fully claimed that situation.

That fullness of restoration may be beyond the horizon of our lifetime, or several lifetimes. But the redemption of the world has been set in motion and continues. Our part, as Dykstra's definition of "lived faith" indicates, is "appropriate and intentional participation" in the present chapter of that unfolding process. Seeing a situation with the "double" vision just described is a first step to discerning what our participation in God's ongoing, redemptive work might look like, in the here and now.

There is no single preaching strategy that, by itself, will activate those in our pews to become tactical, faithfully improvisational agents of redemptive hope. But this chapter and the three that follow mark out some crucial starting points for preaching. I begin, in this chapter, with a guiding hermeneutic of *promise-grounded* hope, because I believe this to be prerequisite to all other strategies. Exercising a hermeneutic of promise-grounded hope is one of the deepest "wells" from which Christians need to draw as they seek to bear faithfully improvisational witness to God's love and justice, especially in situations where they have limited power and leverage.

By a *hermeneutic*, I mean an interpretive lens—a viewfinder, or aid to vision, that reveals deep resonances and coherences in that which we are trying to understand. Preachers reflect from time to time on the hermeneutic they bring to Scripture. To reflect on one's biblical hermeneutic is to reflect on the expectations and guiding principles one brings to the task of reading Scripture well, with due attention to its origins, its cultural assumptions, and its major themes and trajectories. I will argue here that a hermeneutical lens of hope, one anchored specifically in the deep biblical tradition of God's character as a maker and keeper of promises—*not* in human, can-do optimism!—is appropriate for interpreting *both* Scripture *and* the realities of everyday life.

The situations those in our pews confront at home and at the workplace—and in their extended family systems, their neighborhoods, and their schools—may seem far from redemptive or holy; yet all the ground of our human existence is holy because the God of redemptive promise has preceded us there. This means that even situations that seem to us utterly God-forsaken can be places of redemptive possibility. In the desolation of the valley of dry bones (Ezek. 37), Ezekiel sees only disconnected bits of human skeletons, the shattered detritus of death's triumph. Yet Ezekiel "prophesies" to the bones. A future-summoning word interrupts the deathly stagnant stillness of the valley. The daring God-given word of the prophet rattles the silence. The bones begin to reassemble, although they are not yet alive. Ezekiel prophesies again—speaks an expectant word, a future-framing word—to that which is unseen, to the Breath. The bones are enfleshed now; they breathe, they stand, and they move. In the valley is a living multitude of those summoned by God out of death into life.

A hermeneutic of hope turned toward the world in our preaching reframes and *limits* that which is deadly and death-dealing. All preaching is, in a sense, Easter preaching—an extension of the claim that death, as well as the fear it inspires, is not ultimate. In light of divine promises, we can dare to imagine differently; and as we shall see later in this chapter, once we have the capacity to imagine differently, we have the capacity to act differently.

This chapter unfolds in three sections—the first and second fairly brief, the third more involved. In the first section, I suggest that divine promises, made and kept, constitute a hope-sustaining thread throughout the canonical Scriptures embraced by Christians. I want to be clear that, in my view, it is *by no means the case* that God's promises in the Old Testament are left suspended, unfulfilled, and incomplete until the witness of the New Testament brings closure. While *some* Old Testament promises remain open ended at the close of the Old Testament canon, and while the New Testament presents itself as testimony to the fulfillment of *some* of those open-ended promises, to reduce the Old Testament to "unfulfilled promise"—little more than a "set-up" for the "fulfillment" of the New Testament witness—is inaccurate. Such a reading also tends to invite supercessionist and anti-Semitic interpretations of the Hebrew Scriptures.

Employing a hermeneutic of promise-grounded hope, one quickly discovers that the Hebrew Scriptures testify as surely as the New to a God who makes and keeps promises. In fact, the sustained motif of divine promises, made and kept, creates arcs of hope and deep-running strands of coherence *within each testament*. This is not to say that the New Testament is dependent on the Hebrew Scriptures. The New Testament is, in many ways, a rereading of the Old. The texts that counted as Scripture for the early Christians are reread in the New, through the lens of Jesus's ministry, death, and resurrection. But those of other faiths also know the God who makes and keeps promises. Christian preachers can preach from the Hebrew Scriptures and bear witness to the God who is a maker and keeper of redemptive promises. Those of other faiths for whom the Hebrew Scriptures are sacred can worship and celebrate the God who makes and keeps redemptive promises.

In the chapter's next section, I will rely, in part, on the work of theologian and homiletician James F. Kay, in order to show how a hermeneutic of promise-grounded hope enables us faithfully to reimagine everyday situations "bifocally" or "stereoscopically."[3] On the one hand, we can face squarely the wreckage that human beings' deceitfulness, greed, and abuses of power have left in their wake. We can name these things for what they are. On the other hand, the arc of redemptive hope created by God's cross-sealed promises of mercy and justice allows us to discern, amid these destructive realities, openings for acts of redemptive resistance.

In the chapter's next section, we turn to the preaching task itself, addressing one central question: How can preaching through an interpretive lens of promise-grounded hope equip our listeners to act in ways that expose and destabilize behaviors, assumptions, policies, and systems that exploit and enslave human beings, as well as God's nonhuman creation? Here, we will trace the dynamics of two sermons that take evil seriously, yet employ a hermeneutic of

3. Kay, "Word of the Cross," 51–54.

promise-grounded hope to reframe our experience and energize us to resist life-diminishing forces.

The chapter closes with three preaching strategies that can equip our listeners to turn toward the world with a hermeneutic of promise-anchored hope, able to face up to the brokenness of the world, yet daring to bear witness to the redemptive love and justice of God in everyday situations.

Divine Promise as Interpretive Lens: Rereading Both Word and World

The God to which the Christian canon attests—Hebrew Scriptures as well as the New Testament—is a maker and keeper of promises. Thus, choosing *promise-grounded hope* as an interpretive lens for understanding both Scripture and the world of experience is by no means arbitrary. The prominence of divine promise, and the hope-infused action it inspires, is suggested by the structure of Scripture itself.

Grammatically speaking, a promise is a commissive. Commissives are forms of speech that create a bond of obligation between giver and receiver; both live within a new arc of expectation. Promises, particularly public promises, have an *illocutionary* effect of creating a new public state of affairs. Speaking a promise of marriage creates a new reality (a marriage). When a mortgage is signed, promises are made by both homeowner and lender. Promises establish new relationships. Promises also restructure time. They are the sorts of statements that create a new *experience* of time—namely, an arc of expectation that connects every present moment to a future horizon, a not-yet-realized state of affairs. Promises, therefore, not only change the way we experience the present (perhaps with greater patience, or greater impatience!); promises also change how we assess the appropriateness of one or another course of action in the present.

Consider the difference that an engagement to be married makes in the lives of a prospective couple. Welcoming that future shifts each partner's thinking about self, other, and the scope of what counts as family. It has social, legal, and economic implications. Or consider what happens when a young couple discovers they are expecting a child. Suddenly, the future they were anticipating is replaced by a different scenario. A changed future changes how things look in the present. Their trendy, tiny downtown apartment in the arts district is suddenly assessed with altered vision. (Can we really fit the bassinette under the desk?) They see themselves in a new light—as potential parents. They experience a new kinship with shoppers toting boxes of disposable diapers or pushing strollers. A changed future reframes present experience. New possibilities open up. New patterns of action that would have made no sense yesterday make sense today.

The same is true when we reassess the settings and situations of our lives reframed by God's promise to renew all things. In Christian liturgy, divine promises of presence, care, and ultimate healing and freedom ring out in acclamations, prayers, Scripture reading, proclamation, creed, and Table rites. These liturgical reiterations of divine promise reframe present sufferings (and hallow present joys) by taking them up into the vector of a future called *new creation*, already inaugurated in the risen life of Jesus Christ. The saints of history have plumbed the depths of hope to endure suffering and to challenge life-diminishing conditions, defying the powers that keep structures of oppression in place. Those whose hope is anchored in God's promised future—one where the hubris, greed, and indifference of abusive power no longer prevail and where compassion and justice thrive—are emboldened by promise to move into the world prepared to act in terms of that horizon of hope.

Divine promises, made and kept, recur like a deep heartbeat throughout the Christian canon. It is not too much to say that divine promises function as a deep, unifying element amid the vast diversity of canonical materials and the diverse theological perspectives sponsored within the Bible's pages. Divine promises create and sustain arcs of expectation that point beyond the texts themselves, envisioning a far horizon in which justice and mercy will prevail. Generation to generation, the prophets foretell a time when God will redeem and renew the whole created order.

As we noted above, it is too often assumed that God makes

promises in the Old Testament, and none are fulfilled except when Jesus appears in the New Testament. This is far from true. Again and again, the God of Abraham and Sarah, Isaac and Rebekah, Jacob and Leah and Rachel, Moses and Aaron and Miriam, Gideon and Deborah, Ruth and Amos and Isaiah, and Jeremiah and Daniel and Esther makes promises and then—sometimes centuries later—fulfills them. God's promise to lead God's people to "a land to dwell in" is deferred during four hundred years of slavery in Egypt, delayed for forty years in the wilderness, and ultimately fulfilled.

Within that overarching trajectory of expectation, other promises are made and kept. Among them are the story of God's promise of an heir to Abraham and the promise to make of Hagar's son Ishmael a great nation. There is God's promise to Moses to change Pharaoh's heart and deliver the Hebrew slaves, and then the promise to sustain Joshua, despite the demise of the rest of his generation, until he can lead the people across the Jordan. Generations later, God's promise of a son to the once-barren Hannah is kept in the birth of the prophet Samuel. God's promise to raise up a king after God's own heart is made and kept within the span of Samuel's ministry.

The divine promises of the Bible are often double-edged. Sadly, the oft-repeated promise that the nation will be undone if it continues to be double-minded in its worship is kept; yet this is balanced by the promise of God to lead the people back to their land. This promise, too, is kept within the range of the Old Testament witness.

The New Testament bears witness to the incarnation, God's entry into historical time in Jesus of Nazareth. This event is interpreted as the inauguration of God's promise of radical redemption and renewal that will ultimately involve all of creation. The New Testament testifies that this promise is kept in the life, death, and risen life of Jesus Christ. The promise of all things made new remains open ended. It is still being kept in and beyond the church, through the work of the Spirit. We live within the arc of hope this open-ended promise creates. Passages such as Romans 8:18-21 indicate that this promise of world-renewal includes not only human beings but all that makes up creation. Romans echoes far older promises to this effect, as we find in such passages as Isaiah 65:17-25.

In the New Testament, as in the Hebrew Scriptures, there are promises made and kept over shorter spans of time. Mary is promised that she will bear a child who will be the savior, and that takes place. She is also promised that a "sword will pierce" her soul; that, too, takes place. Jesus promises that he will depart from his disciples but later return to them. That promise, too, is kept. The promise of the outpouring of the Spirit, attested in Joel 2:28–29, is renewed and made more specific by Jesus during his ministry. It is fulfilled, according to Christian interpretation, at the Feast of Pentecost in Jerusalem, and on subsequent occasions in Acts, with every indication that this outpouring is ongoing into the present.

The Relationship of Different Biblical Genres to the Thread of Promise

God's promises are not presented in Scripture as isolated contractual statements. They are embedded in, and assumed by, the full range of canonical materials. Like the sturdy woof strands on a loom (running lengthwise throughout the weave), God's promises carry the weft threads—stories, wisdom texts, prophetic oracles, and apocalyptic visions—and draw these elements into a coherent pattern of expectation and hope.

The dozens of stories within the canonical texts—extended sagas as well as brief vignettes—reiterate, clarify, test, or even cast shadows of ambiguity upon divine promises. We learn through these stories the struggle of communities and individuals of the past with divine promises of blessing or judgment; much like us, they gamble on other ways of seeing and navigating their world. Despite very real tensions among various biblical portraits of the divine nature, biblical storylines overwhelmingly attest to the faithfulness of God to God's promises. Arcs of promise draw biblical narratives into patterns and continuities. Prime examples are the stories of the patriarchs, which detail the fulfillment of God's promise to establish a people unique in their vocation to bless the world in God's name.

Functioning as a rhetorical link, of sorts, between divine promises and the tradition's narratives are creedal texts. Old Testament scholar Patrick D. Miller draws our attention to the work of Hermann Spieckermann on a recurring ancient creedal formula found in Exodus 34:6-7 and echoed elsewhere in Scripture. Described by Spieckermann as the governing *leitmotif* of the Old Testament, this creed declares, "The Lord, the Lord, a God merciful and gracious, slow to anger, abounding in steadfast love and faithfulness, keeping steadfast love for the thousandth generation, forgiving transgression and iniquity and sin . . . but by no means clearing the guilty."[4] As if standing back from the wide canvas of sacred history, a canvas bordered by promise and filled with narrative detail, the psalmist celebrates the constancy of divine mercy and forgiveness without limit, mysteriously coupled with divine determination to take seriously the iniquitous abuse of the material world and human community by the powerful, the greedy, the arrogant, and the self-absorbed. This recurring creed gives substance to the character of the promiser.

Other biblical genres, as well, resonate with the canonical core of promise. Divine promises, as well as the trustworthiness of their maker, are celebrated in covenant-renewal rites. Biblical wisdom both teaches and ponders the content, reliability, and scope of divine promises, as well as the consequences of living either in light of those promises or indifferent to them. Divine promises are brought to bear on social, political, and economic realities in prophetic oracles; they are interpreted and reinterpreted as the nation finds itself in new historical circumstances.

Certainly, other bases for construing canonical unity have been proposed. A prominent one since the 1970s, as noted in chapter 1, has been to construe Scripture as fundamentally representing a single, unified story of God.[5] But close examination of biblical nar-

---

4. Patrick D. Miller, *The Lord of the Psalms* (Louisville: Westminster John Knox, 2013), 64, 75.

5. Consider, for example, the work of theological ethicist Stanley Hauerwas. Hauerwas tends to speak in terms of *the* story when referring to Scripture—a practice that has the effect of "saming" differences among the reading strategies of communities in different social locations and of dismissing other possibilities for construing the coherence of the canon. Hauerwas argues from his univocal reading of *the* story of the people of God to quite particular and determinate practices (non-

ratives makes this construal of unbroken narrative unity difficult to sustain at points. An advantage of reading Scripture through a hermeneutical lens of promise-grounded hope is that it allows us to acknowledge the presence of difference, tension, and multiple perspectives within the canon. Scripture's narratives can be read as both carriers of, and commentary upon, a central cable woven of divine promises—made and kept or yet to be kept. This approach to biblical narratives honors more fully the complicated diversity of biblical stories, without sacrificing Scripture's canonical coherence.

The canon, after all, is not a systematic theology. It is a robust and open-ended conversation (and even contestation) carried on among people living in relationship to a divine promiser. Scripture records how these people struggled to interpret the vicissitudes of their lives, as they lived within the arcs of expectation created by divine promise. We, like our forebears, struggle to understand and respond to the divine maker of those promises.

Ultimately, the most consistently reiterated testimony of the canonical "library" is that God, the maker and keeper of world-altering promises, is worthy of worshipful trust.

Reenvisioning Everyday Situations Bifocally

Adopting a hermeneutic of promise-grounded hope in preaching means that we read not only biblical texts, but also the settings and situations we encounter in everyday experience, through the interpretive lens of divine fidelity. This hermeneutic in preaching grants—first to the preacher, but also, over time, to her listeners—a bifocal, stereoscopic view of the concrete realities with which we grapple.[6]

Homiletical theologian James F. Kay points us to 2 Corinthians

---

violence, for example) as necessarily and exclusively consonant with the character and actions of God portrayed in this single canonical story. See *The Peaceable Kingdom: A Primer in Christian Ethics* (Notre Dame: University of Notre Dame Press, 1983).

6. I develop bifocal vision somewhat differently than does James Kay, accenting the arc of expectation as created by promise rather than by apocalyptic.

5:16–17, which indicates something of the bifocal vision that is ours, thanks to living within the arc of divine promises, made, kept, and still awaiting fulfillment in Jesus Christ.

On this side of the cross, according to the apostle Paul, we no longer understand Jesus Christ as merely human—that is, as nothing more than the victim of the old-aeon powers of sin and death. At the cross, in Jesus's dying, "everything old has passed away," or is as good as dead. Even if the old-age norms appear to prevail— the spoils appear to go to those who amass riches, and those who threaten and abuse appear to win—the grip of those powers on the human future will not last forever. The cross, which is *defeat* of its victim from the world's point of view, is from the divine viewpoint the defeat of death itself and of every power that imagines that it can prevail through the threat of death.

The cross, therefore, is the point at which God's promised future overtakes the brokenness of the present, engendering the peculiarly "bifocal" or "stereoscopic" vision of Christian faith. Paul declares the new reality the cross discloses: "If anyone is in Christ, there is a new creation!"—or, literally, "behold!—*new creation!*" This is not a dispassionate observation; this is a cry of glad astonishment evoked by the bifocal *revelation* of the future of God overtaking the brokenness of the human condition. The church's testimony points to two strong pieces of evidence that this promise of God is already on its way to fulfillment: the risen life of Jesus Christ and the outpouring of the Holy Spirit, who has by no means left, but continues to work in both church and world to break down what impedes that future and to promote what nourishes it.

God's promise ultimately to defeat the powers of evil and bring to completion the "new creation," of which Jesus Christ himself is the forerunner, empowers us with bifocal vision that changes our experience of present reality.

First, bifocal vision grants us the courage to see things for what they are. It may seem paradoxical that a hermeneutic of promise-grounded hope becomes a lens for identifying what is evil and destructive. But, truth be told, we often lack the courage to see and name evil for what it is; we need a cushion of denial if all we have to go on is a capacity for sprightly optimism.

It is significant that the bifocal vision of promise-grounded hope frees us not only from fear but also from the obligation to buoy ourselves up with false, self-generated optimism. We are able to come to grips with the destructive dynamics at work in the world and admit that their tentacles may reach into our places of work and learning, into the structures of government that affect us every day, and may reach even into our own family systems. Bifocal vision equips us to face squarely the grip of fear, racism, and greed around the globe and in our own hearts and minds. We can identify the deadly proliferation of fear-mongering portraits of "the other" that feed on popular myth and stereotyping, made yet more toxic when justified in the name of "family values," the economic stability of the community, or nationalism.

Ultimately, the bifocal vision granted us by God's promise of a redeemed future not only allows us to see the present with un-varnished realism but also allows us to reassess present situations *as they will be* in light of God's future. We're able to discern the inbreaking of the Spirit's redemptive work, and then risk (quoting Dykstra again) "appropriate and intentional participation in the redemptive activity of God."

Granted the gift to see not only what is, but also what *can* be and *will* be, we gain courage to analyze with open minds ways that we may be complicit—sometimes unintentionally and unwittingly—in supporting unjust systems of social control. We can call out unholy uses of power not only in the world, but also in the church. We can raise the alarm when populations are written off as worthless, disposable, or inherently untrustworthy. We stand alongside men, women, and children who have been targeted, simply because of the color of their skin, for aggressive policing, unwarranted detain-ment, and disproportionate imprisonment in the name of "law and order"—fodder for a growing and prosperous incarceral industry.

We see, speak, and act against systematic injustice within the arc of redemptive hope. God's promise to renew all things through inclusive love, radical mercy, and restorative justice emboldens us to become agents of redemptive interruption willing to chal-lenge existing conditions with Spirit-driven tactics that call into question business as usual. Bifocal vision allows us to see not only what is, but also the redeemed, renewed future, begun in the risen Christ, whose light reaches into the darkest corners of the world's travail.

Divine Promise, Imaginative Rehearsal, and Action

Paul Ricoeur (1917–2005), one of the most prominent philosophers of the twentieth and twenty-first centuries, sought to clarify the connections between imagination and action. Imagination, he argued, is the essential precursor to action in any situation. "Without imagination," wrote Ricoeur, "there is no action."[7] The actions we pursue, in other words, are "rehearsed" first, in imagination.

Sometimes, this work of experimental, imaginative "rehearsal" is so instantaneous and automatic that we barely notice it. Other times, especially when we are wrestling with multiple options of considerable consequence in difficult situations, our imaginative rehearsals are quite self-conscious and prolonged. Either way, says Ricoeur, "it is imagination that provides the milieu, the *luminous clearing*, in which we can compare and evaluate motives as diverse as desires and ethical obligations."[8] I would add that imagination is the "luminous clearing" in which our listeners can reimagine the troubled and troubling situations of their everyday lives through a lens of hope, anchored in God's determination to redeem all things. To invite listeners into that "luminous clearing" is one of the most crucial moves in Christian preaching.

Historically, though, theologians have disparaged imagination. Some speak of it as the devil's own tool, luring the unwary deeper and deeper into temptation. They deny any positive role for imagination. Yet, since the mid-nineteenth century, an increasing number of literary scholars and moral theorists have contended that imagination is indispensable to ethical discernment and action. The exercise of imagination is what allows us to discover that some courses

---

7. Paul Ricoeur, *From Text to Action: Essays in Hermeneutics, II* (Evanston, IL: Northwestern University Press, 1991), 177.

8. Ricoeur, *From Text to Action*, 177.

of action do not lead to desirable ends, while others do. Imagination is fundamental to creative innovation and improvisation.

It is important to recognize that when we talk about "imagining" in a theological context, we are not talking about make-believe—pretending that the world is a particular way when we are well aware it is not. We are talking, instead, about the human capacity to entertain possible states of affairs, and to "try out" different patterns of action to achieve specific aims in anticipated situations. Recent studies in the field of cognitive development suggest that imagination is, in fact, essential to the healthy emotional and cognitive development of human beings. The work of British psychologist D. W. Winnicott focused on imaginative play in the development of very young children. Through close observation of infants playing near their mothers, Winnicott learned that infants who were allowed to play with objects in safe space, and to do so without unnecessary oversight or interference from their caregivers, tended to be bolder and more inclined to explore and risk new things than infants whose mothers closely supervised and directed their play.

In the "transitional space" of imaginative play, Winnicott theorized, differentiation gradually develops between the infant's own bodily and emotional self and that of the mother and the external world. The young child gradually gains knowledge of the world, develops a healthy attachment to and differentiation from significant others, and develops the courage to act within and upon the external world.[9]

Winnicott theorized that play develops the human capacity to entertain "illusion." For Winnicott and those who have gone on to develop his ideas, illusion refers neither to make-believe nor to being deceived into thinking that something is there that really is not (as in seeing a mirage on the horizon). Illusion refers to the way that our brains imaginatively construct and test hypothetical states of affairs and rehearse possible actions and their consequences.

Homiletician and preacher Peter J. M. Henry has argued that imagination—particularly the capacity to construct and test "illusion"—is best thought of as a "shared project" between preacher

9. See D. W. Winnicott, *Playing and Reality* (London: Tavistock, 1971).

and listeners. The event of preaching, Henry argues, is not one-way communication, but a dialectical process in which listeners integrate into their own experience what they are hearing. This process is enhanced, Henry argues, when we make space in the sermon for imaginative rehearsal of the courses of action that the gospel projects into the world of everyday experience. Following Winnicott's lead, Henry calls this move of imaginative rehearsal for action in the world "constructive or creative illusion."[10]

Too often, preachers bypass this crucial step of entertaining possible courses of action. Instead of pausing to muse with the congregation on the possibilities to which a biblical text points (in the mood of "What if—?" or "What would it look like—?"), the preacher explains the text and then, in a rising tone, spits out a series of interrogations ("Don't we often fail to . . . ?" "Are we not guilty of . . . ?" "When will we get serious about . . . ?"), followed by a string of moral exhortations ("It is up to us to . . ." and "Therefore, we must—!"). Listeners have no chance to invest their own imaginative energy in making connections between the biblical text being preached and the realities of their everyday lives—lives that they, clearly, know and understand better than we ever will. Imagination, far from being an escape from real-world action, plays an essential role in producing real-world action.

"Imagining in preaching," writes Henry, "has a *telos* beyond the immediate sermon, *namely, to engender further faithful imagining.*"[11] In the course of the sermon, "preacher and community share an

10. Peter J. M. Henry, "Shared Imaginings: The Understanding and Role of Imagination in Contemporary Homiletics" (unpublished dissertation, Princeton Theological Seminary, 2009), 180.

11. Henry, "Shared Imaginings," 206; italics added. Henry summarizes seven "distinctives" of his theological theory of imagining in preaching, as follows: "(1) imagination is not something we have but instead imagining is something we do; (2) from beginning to end, preaching is an imaginative activity and imagining is not just a tool to be wielded as needed; (3) imagining in preaching involves multiple parties; (4) imagining in preaching has a telos beyond the immediate sermon, namely to engender further faithful imagining; (5) imagining and preaching are embedded in worship and therefore impacted by the totality of the worship experience, especially liturgy and music; (6) all forms of speech and preaching, not just poetic or dramatic, involve imagining; and (7) imagining in preaching plays a

illusion in order to organize and interpret experience, so that they may respond faithfully to the living God whose relationship with them and the world generates an ongoing dynamism."[12]

Sermons That Generate Bifocal Vision

Here we examine two sermons that employ the kind of stereoscopic vision that, on the one hand, faces squarely a situation of horror, death, and the temptation to despair yet, on the other, dares to declare that God's ultimate promise of redemption and renewal holds us fast amid the devastation. Reframing the present and the future in hope-generating divine promise, these sermons refuse to hand over the world to the powers of fear, despair, and death.

| NANCY J. DUFF, "GROUND ZERO"[13]

It fell to Nancy J. Duff, professor of theological ethics at Princeton Theological Seminary, to preach at the opening retreat for the entering students of the new junior M. Div. class on Sunday, September 16, 2001. Five days earlier, on the morning of Tuesday, September 11, two hijacked jets had crashed into the Twin Towers in New York City, a little more than an hour from Princeton. Hours later, horrified onlookers and millions of TV viewers watched these immense skyscrapers crumble to dust. Another plane had been flown into the Pentagon building in Washington, DC, less than three hours' drive south. Still another, diverted from its intended target—possibly the White House—by the courageous, self-sacrificing intervention of passengers, had plunged into a field near Somerset, Pennsylvania, killing everyone on board.

Now, just days later, Professor Duff faced a junior class of deeply

---

role in the openness of individuals and communities to the Word of God and the activity of the Holy Spirit."

12. Henry, "Shared Imaginings," 230.

13. Nancy J. Duff, "Ground Zero" (sermon preached for beginning seminarians, September 16, 2001); personal manuscript used by permission of the author.

shaken young adults, most in their twenties or early thirties. All
of them were wrestling with the shock and gut-wrenching grief
that had taken hold of virtually every US citizen as the footage of
the smoldering Pentagon building, the wreckage in a Pennsylvania
field, and the burning and crumbling Twin Towers played over and
over again on every television set in every household, bar, and train
station, coast to coast.

As she stood to preach, Duff realized that some of these new
students were most probably questioning the trustworthiness of the
very beliefs that had brought them to seminary—that God is good
and powerful, that in Jesus Christ we know a love stronger than hate,
that God has a redemptive future for the world.

The sermon Duff preached that day is a model of rhetorical skill
and theological integrity. It is based on two texts, Ezekiel 37:1–14,
the encounter between Ezekiel and the Lord in the valley of dry
bones, and Matthew 2:7–12, the journey of the magi to the Christ
child. With remarkable and fitting brevity—without a wasted word,
in fact—the sermon comes alongside the listeners in the depths of
dismay and disorientation. Duff then tests and eliminates sources
of false promise and false hope, finally pointing her listeners to the
only source of hope worthy of the name—the God who can call
forth life even in those violence-blasted places, in the world and in
our hearts, where death seems to have triumphed.

Duff's sermon begins with three brief paragraphs, each beginning with the words "Ground Zero." What is "Ground Zero"? It
is, says Duff, "the place where a nuclear bomb hits, . . . the place
where persons and things are made void." "Ground Zero" is "the
place where two hijacked planes crashed into the Twin Towers, . . .
beginning the nothingness that such destruction brings, . . . where
human lives along with human joy and hope have been made void."
"Ground Zero" is "the place that God shows Ezekiel—the valley of
dry bones," a place where "the burden of despair [was] just as heavy,
and all reason for hope just as elusive as we find it now."

In three brief paragraphs, each beginning with two words sound-
ing like the tolling of a bell to honor the dead, Duff names the place
in which her listeners find themselves. Rhetorically, she overlays
three images—Hiroshima, "Ground Zero" in New York City, and

the valley of dry bones in the Ezekiel text—so that each resonates with the others. Notably, Duff will use this rhetorical strategy of triads—a triplet of short paragraphs, sentences, or phrases—no less than seven more times in her sermon. Yet the repetitions do not become tiresome. Instead, they form a reliable, quasi-poetic rhetorical framework on which we, her listeners, may lean in our weary grief. Transitional paragraphs between the triadic structures establish important perspectives on the trouble Duff's listeners are experiencing.

Immediately after the three "Ground Zero" scenes with which she opens, Duff names the core experience that every listener readily recognizes, no matter where they have come from to begin their seminary lives: "Many of us this week have found it almost impossible to tear ourselves away from the television news reports, which were broadcast from ground zero." Next comes a triad, each statement beginning with the phrase "We are watching . . ."—naming what all who lived through those days recall: the obsessive absorption with images and information and infinitely many stories of devastating grief.

Next, having named the tragedy itself, as well as our reactions to it, Duff poses the key question that drives the rest of her sermon: "So, where *do* we look and to whom *do* we listen to find our way from ground zero?"

At this turning point, Duff introduces into the so-far dark-hued landscape of her sermon a pinpoint of light. She quotes Elie Wiesel, who suggests that "if we follow Ezekiel's gaze and listen to his words we will 'feel stronger than death, [and] more powerful than evil,' for we will be rewarded by the conviction that hope is forever founded and forever justified."[14] With this glimmer of hope set on the far horizon, Duff turns to the Ezekiel text to which Wiesel refers, noting that "Can these bones live?" is not a human question addressed to God; "it is *God's* question to Ezekiel. And now it is God's question to us." Employing once again the triadic structure

---

14. Duff quotes Elie Wiesel, "Ezekiel," in *Congregation: Contemporary Writers Read the Jewish Bible*, ed. David Rosenberg (New York: Harcourt Brace Jovanovich, 1987), 167.

that creates the steady heartbeat of her sermon, Duff suggests that God asks that question in Ezekiel's valley of dry bones, God asks it at the "ground zeros" of September 11, 2001, and "whenever we are confronted with human frailty and vulnerability, with human sin and violence, God asks us, 'Can these bones live?'"

With pastoral sensitivity, Duff clears the table of tempting but inadequate answers to God's question about the bones—both the "no" of despair and the too-glib "yes!" which does not "express hope, but cruel naiveté or blind arrogance." Then, with the clear-eyed honesty that was so desperately needed, but sorely lacking, in the early post-9/11 days when militaristic bravado and self-righteous rage filled the airwaves, Duff dismisses, as well, a triad of false answers: trumping violence with still greater violence, scapegoating particular religions or ethnicities, or blind, nationalistic hubris.

In a brief paragraph. Duff shifts our focus to the Matthew text. Again, a triplet of simple affirmations that begin with the phrase, "The star that we follow," signals this turn. The star of our longing will not stop over the US capital (hope lodged in politics), it will not stop over the stock market (hope lodged in economic resurgence), nor will it stop over the Pentagon (hope lodged in military solutions). No!—"the star we follow stops over the manger. . . . Our hope will spring from the ashes not because human power will make it so, but because the child in the manger demonstrates God's power to bring into existence that which was not there before."

Duff's sermon does not leave us by the manger, however. She moves us on, suggesting that, like the magi, we must *return to our country by another road . . .* not under the sign of any nation's flag, not under the burden of despair, but under the star that leads to the manger." Posing one last time the question of the sermon, "Can these bones live?" Duff closes with a final rhetorical triad: "Together we can refuse to give in to despair. Together we can refuse to say, 'yes,' based on a human vision. Together we can say in faith, 'O God, thou knowest!'"

On that day, Duff preached a sermon that refused to soothe fear with shallow optimism or encourage misplaced confidence in purely human stratagems. Instead, she reframed both the horrors we had all witnessed on our television sets, as well as the deep disquiet in our souls that those images had inspired, in divine promise. We are in the hands of a God whose nature it is to bring life out of desolate valleys of bones and ashes.

> Timothy F. Simpson,
> "We Are Called to Be an Eastering Presence"[15]

On Easter Sunday, 2015, at Lake Shore Presbyterian Church in Jacksonville, Florida, Rev. Timothy Simpson did what every preacher does on this festival day of the church: he preached the good news of Easter. The sermon—based on the short ending of the Gospel of Mark (16:1–8), with its disconcerting final words, "they said nothing to anyone, because they were afraid"—proclaims that God has denied death the last word; God has "Eastered" us and all the world, no matter what we may or may not have to say about it.

The sermon is bracing, even for those of us who were not there. It would be bracing even if we did *not* know that this was Tim's last sermon and that, just two days later, he would die of metastatic kidney cancer (17, introductory note to sermon). Simpson makes no reference to his impending death. Was he afraid? Possibly. But if he was afraid, or if he wasn't, we know this: As he faced that "last enemy," Tim Simpson was not silent about the resurrection of Jesus Christ.

Simpson begins by going straight to the strange ending of the Gospel of Mark, "one of the most interesting passages in all of Scripture about Easter." In fact, says Simpson, the fact that Mark's Gospel ends with fear instead of glad proclamation, or at least some indication of joy, was disturbing even to the early church—so disturbing that, as manuscript evidence reveals, eager writers set about to fix it. Simpson describes some of the surviving literary efforts (known as alternative endings of Mark), none very satisfactory.

---

15. Timothy F. Simpson, "We Are Called to Be an Eastering Presence," *Journal for Preachers* 39, no. 3 (2016): 17–19. In the paragraphs that follow, page references from this work are given in parentheses in the text.

"But," says Simpson, returning to the well-attested, abrupt, fearful ending, "the Gospel ends on *this* note, and I think it's wonderful, even though, in the church, we try to get out of it." We prefer the way other gospels tell it, Simpson observes, "but sorry, you picked the wrong Easter to come to church. You get the Gospel of Mark's ending" (17).

Simpson proposes to his listeners that, palatable or not, Mark's ending "is instructive . . . the women have a point." They have witnessed an execution, seen Jesus "pulled down from that awful place, a bloody mess, torn to pieces . . . put in a tomb." When three days later, "there's a guy standing at his grave saying: 'Oh, he's not here. He's alive. And he's called a meeting at the Starbucks in Galilee for later this afternoon,' would *you* believe it?" No, says Simpson. You are not ready for anything like this. "Man, you'd just get in your car and go home. You'd say, I'm not even going to go there." You'd be more inclined, muses Simpson, to "go back home, take another Ambien, crawl under the covers, go to sleep, and hope that you don't wake up until late in the evening."

Why? "Because if that guy is alive, if that guy is not dead anymore, and the dead are raised, my goodness, what else in the world is going to happen? What else am I going to be facing today? . . . If the dead aren't going to remain in their tombs, then everything may be about to change, because that is precisely how the Scripture presents the resurrection of Jesus" (17).

One great strength of this section of Simpson's sermon is its frankness and its colloquial tone. This is Starbucks conversation, "forgeddabouddit" talk. Simpson has captured the tone of streetside incredulity and avoidance toward an idea that, if true, would put so much of what we base our lives on at risk that it's practically beyond contemplating. Simpson, having rhetorically drawn up a chair beside us, introduces the proposal that will carry the sermon through to its end:

> I've told you before, I preach the same sermon every year on Easter about Walter Brueggemann's suggestion that we consider *Easter* a verb. I know you forget it around the fall of every year, so I bring it up again every spring. (18)

If you believe that "*Easter* is a verb, that God is in the business of Eastering," declares Simpson, then

> the things that you imagine going on in the world aren't going to last. If the dead aren't going to remain in their tombs, then maybe the poor aren't going to stay poor. Maybe the sick aren't going to stay sick. Maybe the disenfranchised aren't always going to be that way.

Simpson invites us to some further imagining of ways that God's "Eastering" of the world may yet unfold. And yet, he avers, "If you really take that seriously, you might just be a little bit afraid" (18).

Afraid, says Simpson, because if Eastering is going on, it might sweep away with it some things we'd rather keep. One of the church's strategies for handling Easter, Simpson suggests, is to "build a firewall" around Easter so that "Easter has to do with Jesus and with us going to heaven." Thus, "we don't allow our faith to spill over into those other places" (at the level of empires, big business, and social change) "where God wants to be an Eastering presence and where God intends to use you and me as Eastering presences out there in the world" (18).

In his concluding move, Simpson declares that "we've been touched by that empty tomb to be an agent of change in the world spreading the good news that . . . it is God's good intention for the entire world to be Eastered."

The final sentences of the sermon are a ringing charge to his congregation, "a community called into being as a new community of hope gathered around the love of God and the love of neighbor, believing that Easter should flow out from this place . . . out into the world around us . . . God's transformation is for everyone and everything." The sermon's final line places the congregation's present and future squarely within the framework of divine promise: "May God help us to live into that promise this day and every day, as we await the coming of the resurrection in all its forms" (19).

For Timothy Simpson, that promised transformation came just two days later.

In this, his final sermon, Simpson is honest about the disconcerting nature of the text, pointing like an arrow to the disturbing reality of resurrection itself. With turns of phrase as accessible and colloquial as coffee-shop conversation, Simpson captures, simultaneously, the discomfiting disturbance and energizing hope of taking seriously God's ongoing "Eastering" of the world. Ultimately, on this poignant Easter morning, Simpson turns the focus of his congregation away from his own condition. He asks them to look out into the world, prepared to seek there the fissures and cracks in "business as usual"—invitations to join the "Eastering" God in the work of transformation. Simpson's final pastoral act is to challenge his listeners—the regulars and the Easter-only visitors, too—to become participants in the Spirit's Eastering of the world.

Preaching Strategies: Building Dynamics of Promise-Grounded Hope in Sermons

Committing ourselves to reading word and world through a lens of promise-grounded hope will change the theological structure, language, and content of our preaching. Briefly, adopting a hermeneutic of promise-grounded hope as we connect the biblical text with our listeners' experience will have three consequences.

First, it will change the theological structure of our sermons. We will declare the *divine indicative*—that is, proclaim what God has done, is doing, and promises yet to do for the renewal of all things—*before* we venture proposals about what *humans* can do, or need to be doing, to participate in that renewal. Rhetorically, beginning with the announcement of divine action and promise makes our sermons less dependent for their momentum on "must," "ought," and "should." Announcing the good news of God's ongoing action in, and commitment to, the world opens the way to the language of invitation, not exhortation: in the light of what God has done and continues to do, what new opportunities open before us?

Second, as Duff's sermon demonstrates, a hermeneutic of hope grounded in divine promise allows us to name bitter realities for what they are. We can create space for lament—*literally* employing the psalmists' language of lament to cry out our dismay. This anguish is real, but the valley of dry bones is not the end of the story. We dare to imagine a world transformed.

Third, we can preach in ways that practice *faithful imagination*, envisioning what can be and will be when God defeats the stratagems of fearmongering, abusive power and establishes a new world of compassion and justice. By exploring fresh visions of hope with our listeners (in the mode of "What if—?" and "What would it be like—?"), we invite our listeners to exercise hope-driven imagination in relation to troubling situations they confront in their Monday-to-Saturday world.

Place the Divine Indicative Ahead of the Human Imperative

For years, I have stressed with my preaching students one principle as a point of departure for both homiletical theology and sermon structure: *"The divine indicative precedes the human imperative."* What this means, theologically, is that the presupposition of any act of human obedience, or any action whereby a Christian bears faithful witness to the redemptive ways of God in the world, is that *God has acted first.* The world is full of tragedy: gross discrepancies between the lives of the rich and the poor, tragic destruction of lives and cultures in ever-more-destructive wars, and tragic waste of irreplaceable resources, thanks to human self-absorption and greed. Yet all the ground is holy, as claimed by the God who is dedicated to bringing life out of death, hope out of the devastation and human hate that avarice produces. God's Spirit continues to work, often unseen. God's ongoing, redemptive work by means of the Holy Spirit in the world is the ground and presupposition of any good that we humans may do. This theological structure in preaching is critically important; it makes divine initiative the motivational presupposition of human initiative, and it changes the language of our preaching from moralistic scolding to eager invitation into God's renewal of all things.

Preaching easily devolves into moralism. Moralism makes the inbreaking of God's reign in the world utterly dependent on human beings' "getting it right." At times, even experienced preachers fall into this trap, resorting at the sermon's close to scolding rather than proclamation of the gospel—which, in essence, is the declaration that God has acted and continues to act in the world. Telling people what they must do *so* God can bless is the negation of gospel. Balancing hope for the world on the shaky foundation of human effort alone implies that God's hands are tied until human beings straighten up and fly right. Such preaching runs counter to the dynamic of genuinely *Christian* hope, which is anchored in God's promises, kept and being kept.

Because love-motivated, gracious promise is the point of departure for every biblical storyline, and for our lives as well, the appropriate, underlying "grammar" of all Christian preaching is to unleash the hope that flows from announcing what God has done, is doing, or promises yet to do. This is not to say that human response to God's promises does not matter. The Scriptures sound, again and again, the divine summons to live in light of God's promises, to discern what God is doing in the world, and to align ourselves with it. In that sense, yes—it is "imperative" that we live in the new reality set in motion by the promises of God. Yet imagining with our listeners what sorts of initiatives are now possible for us, thanks to God's prior, gracious action, is far more likely to inspire faithfully improvisational acts of witness than litanies of "oughts" and "musts."

Keeping the divine indicative ahead of the human imperative in our preaching keeps us, and our listeners, from resting our hope in blithe (and blind?) optimism about human beings' ability to remake the world, if only we can restrain greed and discover the right technology. This is not to say that we should *not* restrain greed and work toward strategies and technologies that level the playing field and widen access around the world to all that makes for human wholeness. It *is* to say that ultimately, Christian hope for the world derives not from human optimism, but from the fidelity of God to God's promises.[16]

16. For a more detailed examination of the difference between human optimism and genuinely Christian hope, see Sally A. Brown, "Hold the Chicken Soup: Preaching Advent Hope," *Journal for Preachers* 30, no. 1 (2006): 10–14. There is a genre of popular literature designed to engender hope through heartening stories with satisfying endings. These stories showcase the capacity of human beings to rise above their circumstances. While this may sometimes be the case, these stories tend to underestimate the degree to which tragedy and devastating loss can rob human

God's open-ended promise to renew all things generates the genuinely Christian hope that sustains us as agents of redemptive action in the world. This dynamic can change our attitude toward the task of preaching itself. Instead of feeling resentful toward a congregation we see as indifferent or resistant to our pleas for action, we can turn to the pulpit eager to declare the good news that we live in an arc of redemptive hope set in motion long ago by our promising God. Instead of dragging ourselves to the pulpit in one more effort to prod or shame our parishioners into action, we turn toward the preaching moment eager to show them, once again, that God has preceded them into the ordinary settings and situations of their lives, and to provide them with the bifocal vision to notice it.

A word of caution is in order here. The way of God in the world is always the way of the cross. The one validated by God on Easter day as firstborn of God's new creation is the one who, in fidelity to the "weak" power of God, defeated death by engaging it fully. The risen Christ bears the marks of crucifixion on his body. Cross and resurrection *together* are God's countermove against all forms of power that seek to maintain the upper hand in this world through intimidation and domination. As Campbell and Cilliers have reminded us, the way of the cross is the foolish way, the liminal way, a path of hope-driven improvisation that risks everything. Intentional participation in the redemptive work of God means following a Lord who has scars on his hands.

Name Realities for What They Are

Reading both Scripture and experience through a lens of promise-grounded hope allows us to see and name situations of suffering and injustice for what they are. We preach to liberate our listeners from the false optimism that has sometimes been forced on Christian believers, as if faith amounted to a refusal to admit that things are as bad as they are.

---

beings of the very capacity for hope. Genuinely Christian hope is anchored not in human resilience or optimism, but divine promise.

Scripture itself resists this notion. The literature of lament comprises better than 40 percent of the psalms and is amply in evidence in other biblical books—nearly all of the prophets, but especially in Jeremiah and Lamentations, and Job. Confidence in the God of promise emboldens us to name the wounds of the world—its myriad sufferers, its deadly conflicts, and the groaning of the natural world. Instead of shutting our eyes and minds to all of this, bifocal vision enables us to face the bitter realities of the human condition and the ecosphere, to weep with those who weep, rage with those who rage, and groan with those who groan. "How long, O Lord?" is the cry of the faithful. In the midst of it, we seek the merciful heart and justice-making hand of the Lord, confident that God has promised that it shall ultimately be otherwise.

Reimagine Concrete Realities through the Lens of Divine Promise

Reframing present situations—ones that are real and immediate, with impact on our listeners—within the hope-generating divine promise of a redeemed future, and then daring to reimagine them, is not an optional flourish in preaching. Yet it is frequently neglected. Most preachers spend far more time decrying the ills of the world and the failures of professed Christians (implicitly the ones in the pews) than they do asking and answering the question, "What could redemption look like in our town's streets, in our homes, in our workplaces?"

This kind of concrete, real-world reimagining is a signature move of biblical prophets. In Christian preaching, concrete, real-world reimagining is an essential means by which we, along with our listeners, discover the "so what?" of the good news our sermon means to declare. Above all, such reimagining is an essential link to action. Just as jazz musicians spend endless hours practicing their musical skills so that they can produce fresh improvisational music, so exercising imagination is a form of "skill practice" for believers who want to respond in faithfully inventive ways to the opportunities and challenges they face in their weekday world.

Such reimagining in our sermons needs to sketch pathways of action that are *realistic and accessible* for those actually sitting in our pews. Nearly as common as scolding at the close of a sermon, and only marginally more helpful, is the ending that fizzles into a series of grand abstractions: Beginning preachers, especially, have a tendency to speak in sweeping generalities when they attempt to imagine patterns of faithful action. "How can we more effectively feed the hungry? Love the unlovable? Show compassion to the lonely?" they ask their listeners. We speak of justice (in general) and compassion (in general) toward (the general category of) the oppressed.

Preachers assume—erroneously!—that the more general their recommendations, the more people will be able to identify with them and fill in the blanks. Actually, the opposite to that is true. The truth is that sketching a *particular* scene of human action in a recognizable setting is always more deeply engaging, persuasive, and imagination-stimulating than dealing in global, general concepts. This skill, usually referred to as *trusting the power of the particular*, can make the difference between sermons that instigate creative action and sermons that only elicit guilt. Say, for example, that the local newspapers have been covering incidents of harassment toward Muslim citizens at malls and theaters in your city. You might tell the story of a "Cultural Pride Day" in an East Coast city where representatives of different ethnicities and distinctive cultures in the city were invited to create floats and march in a parade. Friends of mine who were there watched in dismay when, as a group from western Africa in Muslim dress moved along the street, first one, then several half-full soda cans were lobbed, hard, in their direction. My friends broke out of the crowd on the sidelines and rushed to surround the terrified marchers. Others followed, forming a human shield around them. A scene like this in a sermon puts a face on redemptive hope and prompts us to imagine what it can look like to act as an agent of redemptive hope.

While we do need to ask some questions to get this kind of imaginative work underway, those questions belong in the study, where we ask them of *ourselves*, not in the pulpit where our interrogation is often so rapid-fire that no one, no matter how mentally agile, could possibly answer them all. A better approach is to review the situations of trouble we've identified early in the sermon that cry out for address, then ask ourselves, "What would be happening, or could happen, in this specific situation if we reenvision it as a place where Christian believers have committed themselves to act, trusted the redemptive presence and power of the Spirit?" Painting a vivid brief vignette will generate far more imaginative energy among listeners than a vague gesture in the direction of "injustice" or "human need."

We can return, for example, to the situation described in chapter 1, where Frieda finds herself a party guest among people she does not know well, witnessing a troubling situation. Most of the group is roaring with laughter while an eleven-year-old girl suffers acute embarrassment but is too frightened to protest; this was her father's idea, after all, and she knows better than to contradict him when he drinks. Frieda finds herself increasingly troubled each passing second, but what avenues for tactical, improvisational action are open to her?

Could Frieda interrupt the cruel parody that's taking place by the pool with a parody of her own? This would take courage, verve, and the right tone, but it could be done. But here is the opportunity, the timely "slippage" in this situation: *Frieda, as a stranger here, has the freedom more than anyone else to make a fool of herself; she has the freedom to "get it wrong."* This is an opportunity to undertake action that disrupts and subverts the power dynamics playing out here. It isn't hard to imagine Frieda grabbing someone's hat off his or her head, tilting it over one eye, and running up to the child, yelling, "Fashion police, fashion police!" Exclaiming, "Oh my dear, that suit is just *not* your color!" (and possibly suggesting that the suit would look terrific on, say, Uncle Ralph), Frieda could dress the child with dramatic fuss in a towel—quite probably to the relief of some in the crowd who were actually becoming uncomfortable with the scene but felt powerless to act, maybe held back by their loyalty to (or fear of) the host. Willing to "play the fool," Frieda could give a performance that would be a redemptive interruption, a faithfully improvisational witness to the mercy and justice of God.

Regardless of whether Frieda's playful, improvisational interruption succeeds or fails, she has shifted attention away from the child to herself. She may become the object of anger or scorn; but she has acted as an agent of redemptive interruption. She has changed the scene and changed the subject.

Stories of redemptive possibility are happening all around us, if we keep our eyes open. A student in one of my preaching classes (I'll call him Ned) told about a day when he missed his train to get to his field education job at a church in Trenton. He caught a later train, but he was definitely going to be late for his duties with the youth club at the church. On his way, he passed a homeless man panhandling for change and brushed him off brusquely. But for the rest of the youth-club meeting, Ned was bothered. What sense did it make for a future minister who claimed to care about city folk to dash past that guy? To his relief, the man was there as he headed down the same street to catch the train home.

This time, Ned had filled a bag with food from the youth-group meeting, making sure to include plenty of protein. He offered it to the man, who, to his surprise, brushed *him* off this time—with a curse. Instead of retaliating or giving up, Ned stood his ground and apologized. Stopping to talk with this man would mean missing his train home. He wasn't sure when the next train would come. It was foolish to linger on a darkening city street; and the man was angry, maybe a little drunk. But what mattered at the moment, Ned believed, was reconciliation with this man he had earlier treated as unimportant.

After a minute or two of exchanging words with the man, Ned saw his body relax and his expression soften. The two of them ended up sitting on the steps of an empty building, trading stories and eating the food together. The homeless man, concerned for this young man's safety in the dimming light, walked him to the train.

The things individuals do in ordinary situations matter. Not all the situations that trouble us involve a single individual; sometimes they involve whole systems, and they need to be addressed strategically, in company with others whose voices and presence strengthens our own. Often, we will recognize our opportunity for action in a situation only if we are able to see it stereoscopically—at one and the same time facing the wrongs in the situation squarely, but daring to imagine it from a different perspective, illumined by God's already-begun future of justice and reconciliation.

What we can imagine, we can undertake. Living in the arc of expectation and hope that God's promises create, we can testify with our lives to the inclusive love, radical mercy, and restorative justice of God.

Further Reading:
Preaching Toward the Horizon of Eschatological Promise

Explorations into the unique features and effects of promise-making in human speech and in theology are wide-ranging. Here are a few works that may be especially thought-provoking for preachers.

Hilkert, Mary Catherine. *Naming Grace: Preaching and the Sacramental Imagination.* New York: Continuum, 1997.

Jacobsen, David Schnasa, ed. *Toward a Homiletical Theology of Promise.* Eugene, OR: Cascade, 2018.

Kay, James F. *Preaching and Theology.* St. Louis: Chalice, 2007.

———. "The Word of the Cross at the Turn of the Ages." *Interpretation: A Journal of Bible and Theology* 53, no. 1 (1999): 44–56.

Powery, Luke A. *Dem Dry Bones: Preaching, Death, and Hope.* Minneapolis: Fortress, 2012. See especially chapter 3, "Prophesy to the Bones: Generating Hope through Preaching."

CHAPTER 4

Body Talk: Preaching about
Life-Forming Christian Practices

Behind every agent of redemptive interruption stands a life-shaping community. Because this is true, preachers do well to pay close attention to the life-forming practices of the congregations they lead and to invite the congregation into critical reflection on those practices from the pulpit.

Some readers may wonder why—since we suggested in chapter 1 that a strictly faithful-practices approach to Christian witness has limitations—I would spend a chapter insisting that we preach on Christian practices. There are many reasons; here I will suggest five specific reasons to preach about a congregation's practices of worship, congregational life and decision-making, and public witness.

Why Congregations Need to Hear Sermons
about Their Distinctive Practices

First, to be Christian *is* to participate in a Christian community's shared practices. Christian belief is an embodied participation in shared, meaning-laden actions, not intellectual assent to a set of propositions. Shared Christian practices, as embodied articulations of Christian conviction, orient not only our cognition and emotion, but our bodies—our muscles and our nerves—toward God-given hope. Practices of worship and learning, prayer and conversation, caregiving and justice-seeking form us, bodily, *toward* faith and *in* faith. Agile, faithfully improvisational witness in everyday situations depends, at least in part, on a deep reservoir of kinetic, intuitive, embodied knowing. Sermons that explore the history and current expression of distinctive Christian practices help us make connections among them. Projecting the implications of the things we do *inside* the worship space for our stance toward matters *outside* the worship space helps establish key connections between the life-shaping practices of Sunday and the challenges of Monday and beyond. Members, no less than visitors, would like to know where their community's actions, rituals, and verbal formulas came from and why they look or sound different from one congregation to the next.

Second, thoughtful and critical reflection on a Christian practice from the pulpit is a lively opportunity for *substantive theological reflection* with a congregation. The years I spent in parish ministry, before taking the turn toward academic life, alerted me that often those in the pews have a lot more theological curiosity than we give them credit for. Systematic theology, served straight, can make fairly indigestible sermon fare for all but a hardy few. But unpack the meaning of a Christian practice from the pulpit—with plenty of vivid illustration—and even children and youth may tune in.

Christian practices are not theologically one-dimensional; they are multivalent. This multivalence of meaning in Christian practices is not a weakness or a problem for the preacher; it is an asset. Every Christian practice coordinates a web of related affirmations about the nature of God, redemption, human existence, the shape of Christian hope, and our confidence in God's ongoing, redemptive engagement with the wider world. Whether we are focusing from the pulpit on a practice of worship or one having to do with the congregation's fellowship life, decision-making processes, or service to its community, our practices mediate theological claims, both to us and to those who observe what we do. Critical reflection on a practice allows us to explore the implicit theological meanings that our actions declare. By exploring the specific, local expression of a practice as it plays out in our own congregation, we can also surface anomalies in our practices, or tensions between what we say we believe and what actually happens in our practices. Do we say that women and men have been called by God, equally, to leadership in the body of Christ, when over 70 percent of the time, all the leadership in the chancel at worship is male? Do we claim to welcome all, but unwittingly make some of our buildings, or spaces within them, inaccessible to those with mobility issues? (The front platform of many churches is wheelchair inaccessible.)

Third, in the faith experience of most of us, the process of adapting our bodies and voices to the shape and sound of Christian worship practices is temporally and logically prior to conscious belief. One needs only to watch a three-year-old beginning to imitate the worship postures of adults around her to recognize this. Hymnal on her lap, she may not be singing the same tune as the rest of us, but she is coordinating her body with what is happening around her. Our bodily participation in practices of Christian faith begins *before* we mature, either in years or in understanding, to a point when we're ready to signal our cognitive and emotional embrace of the theological affirmations those practices mediate.

Even if our first experiences with Christian practices began only in adulthood, we begin by figuring out when to stand and when to sit, when to kneel (or not), how to find and follow the text of a hymn, how to move with the music of praise or respond vocally to the preacher, and how responsive litanies work. In other words, we coordinate ourselves with *shared actions* of faith before reaching a state of critically alert, *cognitive* commitment to the meanings these actions mediate. It may, in fact, be the case that someone in our congregation joined up with a mission group to serve a disaster-struck community long before he or she explored worshiping with the congregation, much less before making a profession of faith or becoming a member.

Because bodily participation precedes cognitive assent, the preacher's reflection from the pulpit on a few of a congregation's characteristic shared practices is a more broadly accessible point of entry into theological reflection than shared creedal formulas or confessional statements. Such statements may be obscure to many members, to say nothing of visitors. This is not to say that such statements aren't worthy of sermons; but as springboards for theological reflection, shared practices may provide a better starting point. A pastor reported to me that one of his most eagerly received sermon series went under the simple title "Why Do We Do That?" As French ethnographer Pierre Bourdieu notes, only by means of careful critical reflection are we able to "figure out the meaning of what one has been doing, why one does it, and what it implies."[1] If there is a "time for children" in a service, why not spend that, too, in the "why-do-we-do-that?" mode?

A fourth reason for preaching on Christian practices from time to time is that critical reflection (in the sense of curious exploration) about the specific practices and habits of a local congregation can help its members grasp an important feature of social practices in general: *Our practices are embedded in, and shaped by, their cultural contexts.* Christian practices, theologian Kathryn Tanner reminds us, "cannot be understood in abstraction from their tension-filled relations with the practices of the wider society in which Christians live."[2] In fact, "Christian practices seem to be constituted in part by a slippery give-and-take with non-Christian practices; indeed they are mostly non-Christian practices—eating, meeting, greeting—done differently, born again, to unpredictable effect."[3]

While some will always contend that their community's practices are nothing short of gesture-for-gesture, word-for-word, embodiments of what Scripture teaches in every detail, such a claim ignores the gap between written discourse and embodied enactment, to say nothing of the gap between, on the one hand, ancient texts and the cultures from which they emerged and, on the other, modern human communities' practices. The relationship between a Christian community's practices and its authorizing texts is usually negotiated along the lines of some set of interpretive rules. These rules are usually more implicit than explicit, and how to negotiate this interface is often an issue for debate.[4] Truth be told, a congregation's

1. Pierre Bourdieu, *The Logic of Practice* (Stanford, CA: Stanford University Press, 1990), 232.

2. Kathryn Tanner, "Theological Reflection and Christian Practices," in *Practicing Theology: Beliefs and Practices in Christian Life*, ed. Miroslav Volf and Dorothy Bass (Grand Rapids: Eerdmans, 2002), 231.

3. Tanner, "Theological Reflection," 230.

4. For work that builds in varied ways on the relationship of Christian texts and local practices, see the essays in Nancey C. Murphy, Brad J. Kallenberg, and Mark

practices will usually comport in some fashion with its written texts and traditions, but they will unavoidably undergo adaptation, over time, to local cultural, ethnic, and even class-based norms.

Fifth, preaching about a Christian practice is a chance to *put the congregation's ways of worship and witness into historical perspective.* It may be fair to say that worship practices are slower to change than the more "peripheral" practices of a congregation—its ways of engaging the surrounding community or ways of educating children; yet even the briefest perusal of the history of Christian worship practices puts us on notice that the notion of "unchanging" worship is a mythical beast. Congregations can find it eye-opening to learn that the way they've "always" observed Communion, baptism as they've "always" done it, and the hymns they've "always" sung are the products of slow cultural evolution and theological negotiation, and that it should be no surprise that these dynamics continue to affect Christian worship today. Putting practices into historical perspective can help lower anxiety about worship change.

Sometimes, the process of adapting Christian practices to a new or changing context can yield surprising results. A striking example comes from Papua, New Guinea. When Christian missionaries brought their faith to that culture, they soon discovered that New Guineans had no animal called "sheep" or even "goat." The nearest four-footed, locally recognizable mammalian equivalent to a "lamb" was the pig. This led mission workers in that cultural setting to translate John the Baptist's announcement of Jesus's arrival at the Jordan, "Behold, the 'pig' of God!" Scandalous as that may sound to Western ears, mission workers concluded that the dynamic equivalence of the pig in that culture to the lamb or sheep in ancient Jewish culture made "pig" the best vehicle for the theological meaning intended.

There are dozens of less dramatic examples, of course. In many cultures, the "bread" of Communion is tarot root or rice cakes. A former student told me about a remarkable adaptation-to-context:

Thiessen Nation, eds., *Virtues and Practices in the Christian Tradition: Christian Ethics after MacIntyre* (Harrisburg, PA: Trinity Press International, 2003).

a priest ministering amid severe drought conditions baptized infants with their parents' tears.

Congregational Practices: An Overview

What range of practices should we consider addressing from the pulpit? Typically, a Christian congregation's practices fall into five categories: (1) practices of worship, (2) practices of education and formation, (3) fellowship-building and caregiving practices, (4) practices of public service and witness, and (5) practices of discernment and decision-making.

Practices of worship are a good place to start. These lie, practically and theologically, at the core of a congregation's week-to-week life and give expression to its distinctive identity. Since worship practices articulate most specifically a congregation's understandings of human-divine relationship, practices of worship have implications for all of its other social practices. A congregation's worship practices can be thought of as the turning *hub* of a wheel; they are central to the congregation's life and deliver *centrifugal* energy outward toward the rim of the wheel—the interface between the congregation and its surrounding community. The rest of the congregation's social practices radiate, like spokes of the wheel, from the energizing hub of worship. Practices of volunteer service and caregiving, fellowship and formation, and decision-making and service translate the vision expressed in the community's prayer, praise, proclamation, and sacramental life (font and Table) into forms of shared action that shape many spheres of life.

Second, nearly all congregations devote time and energy to deliberate practices of faith-formation. As we've indicated above, *all* of a congregation's practices, as embodied mediation of core convictions, are profoundly faith-forming at an embodied, kinetic level. Yet specific educational practices help a community's members develop a clearer sense of the coherence of different beliefs with one another and allow them to test the implications of core faith-affirmations for their own lives and for thinking about public issues. Faith-formation practices include formal catechesis for youth members and seekers of faith, educational programs for all ages, and groups that convene through the week to study Scripture or engage other writings on topics of concern to church members. Also in this category would be different forms of spiritual direction for groups or individuals, provided either by pastoral staff or by trained lay spiritual directors.

A third set of Christian practices function to build ties of fellowship and caregiving within and beyond the congregation. Gatherings, particularly around meals or to celebrate significant events in the congregation's life, have been characteristic of Christian communities since the church's beginnings. Other practices are focused on providing care to members and others in crisis situations of illness, bereavement, sudden job loss, or other life-altering events. Sometimes the dynamics of caregiving and fellowship combine; examples that come to mind are a team of members trained to support the congregation's bereaved individuals and families, or a caregiving respite team that helps members or nonmembers with the fulltime care of an Alzheimer's patient or severely disabled family member. Common dedication to a task generates lasting fellowship ties.

Fourth, nearly every congregation engages in practices that bring material support to vulnerable populations in the wider community. Visiting prisoners or, better yet, organizing a joint learning opportunity for those in prison along with church members by creating a video-connected common space are strategies for supporting those persons society has made all but untouchable on common ground. At their best, congregations back up the verbal commitments they affirm in worship with material action, not only calling policy makers and public service systems to account, but also becoming voices for the voiceless and overlooked in their communities. Developing safe winter shelter for homeless citizens, helping refugee families find safe housing and work, and developing transportation networks for aging or disabled residents are all practices that connect Christian communities with other religious and nonreligious groups committed to compassion and justice.

Through such practices, a congregation finds itself working shoulder-to-shoulder with those of other faiths or no professed faith. Foregrounding these shared practices from the pulpit gives the preacher an opportunity to underscore, theologically, the missional tenet discussed earlier in this book—that the *missio Dei* extends beyond the church. The Spirit works in the world, and not only through Christians.

Fifth, undergirding all of the above practices are decision-making practices, both formal and informal. These practices—which typically receive far less attention from the pulpit than they should—are as deeply rooted in a congregation's "DNA" as are its worship practices. That these practices are both formal (recognized in the congregation's governance and records) and informal (operative but not necessarily accounted for in any official policy document or in records) is crucial.

Some congregations have a congregational form of governance (one that is determined internally, by the congregation's membership); others have governance structures prescribed by broader, denominational policies. Yet, in either case, local culture affects profoundly how power is *actually* distributed and exercised in the life of the congregation. Behind and beneath the official policies and flowcharts of the formal decision-making apparatus lie largely invisible networks of allegiance, information, and influence that come to expression at every level of congregational life. In many cases, nothing is intentionally insidious about these information networks; but they can have considerable influence on the way official decision-making power is distributed and used. For example, a congregation's denominational affiliation may be with a body that officially declares that leadership in the church should be equally shared without regard to gender identification; yet entrenched patriarchal cultural norms ensure that the vast majority of the congregation's leaders are men. Elsewhere, an all-too-common scenario may play out in which an "old" family of the church wields disproportionate influence over the selection of the congregation's pastors. The rest of the congregation (what's left of it) simply makes do with the situation, unable or unwilling to confront the hegemonic influence of the inner circle. In another setting, the church's board routinely defers to the opinion of the congregation's biggest giver.

There is perhaps no array of practices more invisible, or more important to explore in preaching, than its ways of distributing power and making decisions. Yet speaking from the pulpit about the patterns and uses of power in a congregation, and who may need to be more empowered, requires having spent enough time in the congregation building trust and openness so that such issues can be brought up with care, fairness, and tact.

As noted earlier, there is considerably more curiosity out in the pews about the things we *do* together, and why we do them, than preachers realize. A few brief advisory notes may help here.

First, particularly when preaching on controversial practices like worship practices or decision-making practices, it makes sense to couple preaching with dialogical opportunities—sermon feedback sessions, panels, and open forums—so that congregation members can raise questions, share their experiences, and express their concerns and hopes.

Second, while historical and theological reflection on how a practice developed, and the theological meanings it mediates, will be appreciated, our forays into history and theology work best mixed with readily recognizable verbal "snapshots"—or literal ones projected on a screen—from the congregational "family photo album." Hands-on involvement in worship, fellowship, caregiving, and mission practices across the whole spectrum of the membership, with special attention to empowering newcomers, children, youth, and older adults, increases everyone's stake in critical reflection on the congregation's shared practices.

Third, when congregational practices are the subject, preaching in the mode of *exploration*, rather than conveying a tone of top-down *explanation*, is most accessible. Many in our pews come from other faith traditions where details of the rites and rubrics of worship, as well as understandings of many other aspects of congregational life, differ from what they experience in our community of faith. Inviting into the room this breadth of experience to be explored and better understood does several things. First, it helps others recognize the diversity of Christian practice, and second, it avoids creating an insider/outsider mentality. Everyone is enriched by a broader view of what it means to be but one part of the body of Christ. As we've indicated, sermons that touch on the *history* of particular Christian practices go a long way to cultivate among the varied generations and social subcultures in the pews an appreciation for the fact that Christianity has always been embedded in, and shaped by, local cultures. Yet, in myriad expressions across geography and time, Christian practices have displayed recognizable continuities and deeply shared commitments.

Why Preaching on Practices Is Crucial to the Everyday Witness of Individual Christians

Becoming an agent of redemptive interruption in one's weekday world requires a reservoir of wisdom, inscribed both in the intellect and in the body. The more we can participate with critical self-awareness in the distinctive practices of Christian communities, the more likely we are to be able to draw on this practical body of knowledge amid the immediacy of everyday situations. Alert participation in an array of shared Christian practices can provide us with a repertoire of action paradigms to draw upon when we encounter challenging situations in everyday spaces.

A colleague tells the story of two congregations that happened to be located right across the street from each other but took very different stances on issues of nonheteronormative sexual orientation and its relationship to church membership and leadership. Their differences showed up with particular clarity on the day the gay pride parade was slated to go right past the front doors of the two face-to-face churches on a Sunday afternoon. On one side of the street, rainbow flags waved. Church members carrying trays of cups with fresh water and portable snacks were poised to refresh the marchers. On the opposite side of the street, postures were stiff, arms were folded, and some held up placards with prominent, condemning messages for the marchers.

The contrast was striking, of course; but what was more striking that day was the behavior of one petite, quite elderly lady from the rainbow flag side of the street holding a tray of cups filled with water. My colleague noticed she wasn't looking at the marchers; she was looking anxiously across the street at the sweating sign holders.

Gripping her tray full of water cups, she set out with determination for the opposite side of the street. Weaving across the street through the startled marchers and all but disappearing somewhere around shoulder-level among the sea of bodies, she was steady as a ship under full sail with her tray of fresh water. Finally, she reached the other side and began handing cups of water to the sign holders and their scowling supporters on the other church's lawn.[5]

This lady must have known, bone-deep, something about bread broken and a cup poured out for the *whole* world, not just some of it.

Preaching about Christian practices can not only help those in the pews become more self-aware participants in those practices, but it can also equip them with embodied, theologically adaptable paradigms to draw upon as they act in faithfully improvisational ways—as did the determined woman with her tray of water cups on that hot day—in new settings and situations.

The next section proposes three specific types of practice-focused sermons that can supply reservoirs of practical, embodied wisdom for those in our pews.

A Plan for Preaching about Christian Practices

Preaching on the Sacraments: Baptism and the Lord's Supper[6]

Regular preaching on the actions of worship, but especially the sacraments (or ordinances) of baptism and the Lord's Supper, establishes deep understandings about God's redemptive engagement with the human project and the material world. Baptism and Communion function, in important ways, to establish the deep structure of *all* Christian practices. We experience in these rites God's promise to renew all things in Jesus Christ, and do so in fully embodied, sensory ways. Linking these sacraments with the public witness

5. O. Wesley Allen, sermon preached at the Academy of Homiletics, November 14, 2015.

6. In some settings, these worship practices are not considered *sacraments*, but *ordinances*.

of the congregation can encourage those in the pews to look beyond the sanctuary walls and, alongside others, become agents of redemptive interruption in everyday life.

Historically and theologically, the practices of Christian baptism and the Lord's Supper establish the animating framework of promise-grounded hope that we discussed in chapter 3. When we preach on the sacraments, we call attention to the deep current that flows through *all* our practices: it is not our own actions, but the initiative and life-giving action of the Spirit that draws us, bodily and kinetically, toward the horizon of God's future.

In baptism, God's redemptive claim upon our lives, as well as that future for which God claims us, becomes the ground and goal of our lives. Of course, every preacher needs to adjust the details of his or her sermons on baptism to the specific understanding of baptism in a particular congregational setting. This needs to be done sensitively, recognizing that some in the pews have come into the congregation from communions that handled baptism differently. That said, baptismal meanings overlap, regardless of the mode and method of baptism. Paul testifies in the opening verses of Romans 6 that we are baptized, by means of water and the Spirit, into the dying and rising of Jesus Christ. This language brings the eschatological horizon of God's future into view at the font and, as I stress in the sermon that follows, brings our ultimate destiny into view when we are either quite new to the world altogether or new to professed faith.

We need to keep in mind as we preach about baptism that—especially in the ancient world—water was not an unambiguously positive symbol. Even in our own time, water is a powerful symbol both of life and death (a fact of which I am reminded, as today's news headlines include reports of nearly one million people in Kerala State, India, displaced by unprecedented flooding, with hundreds of fatalities). The story of the crossing of the Red Sea reflects this dualism; for the escaping Hebrews, it signifies deliverance into a new life of freedom, while for the Egyptians, the Red Sea waters became a tomb.

The Lord's Supper (Holy Communion or Eucharist), like baptism, looks backward to the sin-defeating death of Jesus and forward to feasting in the reign of God, promised both in Old Testament and New Testament texts. Sometimes, Christian communities have lost sight of the future-oriented thrust of the Lord's Supper, reducing its meaning to a memorialization of God's saving work in the past. At the same time, if it is purely a happy meal and not foreshadowed by death, we have lost our bifocal vision.

Early Christian preachers did not hesitate to start with all kinds of texts to preach about baptism and Communion. Thus I often suggest that preachers begin by drawing not just on one or two obvious, go-to texts on baptism or Communion, but work also with an array of different biblical images that can reveal a richer range of theological insight into these core Christian practices. Keeping the biblical resources of our sacramental preaching broad deepens listeners' understanding that sacraments are not univocal in their theological meaning; they are theologically multifaceted.

Yet good sacramental preaching also reaches deeply into the ordinariness of human experience. Satterlee and Ruth suggest that we seek out accessible human experiences that help amplify the theological insights a particular biblical text yields. This move is crucial; it connects our listeners' experience of the sacraments with the ordinariness of the world. Such homiletical crafting underscores that the God who meets us at Table and font meets us, as well, in the world. The alignment of mundane, daily experience with theological insight is what, for Satterlee and Ruth, makes preaching on the core worship practices of baptism and Communion not a pedantic drudgery, but an adventure that points us from the sacramental moment into the everyday world, where an ever-deeper alertness to God's active presence meets us at every turn.

Two Sermons: Baptism and Communion

| A Baptismal Homily, by Sally A. Brown

A baptismal sermon preached at a Presbyterian church was titled "Starting Life at the End of Time," with Romans 6:1–11 as the underlying biblical text. Readers may remember that in this text, Paul reframes baptism in the dying and rising of Jesus Christ. Baptism is being buried with Jesus Christ.

This is how the sermon unfolded. After a lay worship leader had read the epistle selection, I began my sermon with a deliberate repetition of two key lines, verses 3 and 5. From there, I continued,

> Wait a minute—what's with all this death talk? Bringing up death at a baptism is a little like showing up at your best friend's fortieth-birthday party and interrupting the proceedings to read several obituaries of persons who happen to have died on your friend's birthdate the last few years (just to put things into perspective). If there were a wet blanket prize on offer, this would be a way to win it.
>
> And yet the apostle Paul seems to think that bringing up the death of Jesus—a messy public execution, no less!—is highly appropriate baptism talk. In fact, Paul claims that if we want to understand what's going on here today with Charles and Meredith and Laquita [not the real names of the three infants being baptized that day], we've got to stand at the foot of the cross of Jesus and, from there, turn in the direction of his tomb. Because, at least in part, that's what Paul says is happening to these kids today: they are dying with Jesus and going to the tomb with Jesus.

Recognizing, of course, that Paul's two-sided, death/life theological metaphor for baptism would be lost on my listeners unless they understood the ambiguity of water symbolism in the ancient world, I took a moment at this point in the sermon to point out to my listeners what would have been obvious to Paul's first readers but isn't obvious to us:

> Water isn't just all about freshness and washing and thirst quenching and new life; for the ancients, water was a symbol of threat and chaos and the risk of death. Going to sea was a fearsome and unpredictable undertaking. You could end up either at your destination or in a watery grave; it was always high risk.

But this needs to be made sense of, theologically:

> Paul is saying that when the baptismal water touches us, we will surely die . . . but not literally, because Jesus has already undergone death on

our behalf. Having wrestled with the powers of chaos, he went to the depths—"was crucified, died, and was buried," as the creed says—and took down into the deadly waters with him all that is deadly about the way we humans are.

In baptismal homilies, I am always aware that at least a few are there listening, perhaps many—the aunts and uncles and grandparents and friends—who haven't been to church in a long time, or ever. I cannot use standard, insider, "original-sin" talk; I need to make sense of Jesus's fight-to-the-death with death some other way:

Because we do take away life, you know, we human beings. Yes, we look good this morning, we've come to church—but we do deadly things to each other, don't we? With our greed that leads to such deep economic divides that fancy restaurants throw away pounds of uneaten food while a few blocks away someone is dumpster diving for a half-eaten taco. We harbor deadly prejudices and fear, fears that build walls to keep scared people running from death in their home countries from running to ours. Sometimes some of us are so afraid of somebody who looks different, we're willing to shoot first and figure out who they really are and what they are doing later.

Jesus died to overcome the power of our deadly greed and fear to rule us. Jesus broke death's grip on us. He broke death's claim on Charles and Meredith and Laquita by dying and going to the tomb for us, to break, ultimately, their power to hang onto us. You know how he did that? He took us with him, all of us, on that cross and into that tomb.

At this point, it was important that I turn toward the other side of Paul's two-sided metaphor, so I returned to the text.

But you know the very best thing about this? That's not the end of the story.

Hear what Paul has to say about it: "We have been buried with Jesus by baptism into death, so that just as Christ was raised from the dead by the glory of the Father, so we too might walk in newness of

life. For if we have been united with Jesus in a death like his, we will
certainly be united with him in a resurrection like his."

Baptism isn't a death symbol, end of story. It's a been-through-the-
river-already-with-Jesus, newness-of-life symbol.

"So," says Paul—who is probably preaching right here to a bunch
of newly baptized folks—"consider yourselves dead to sin and alive
to God in Christ Jesus!"

Now it was time to connect all of this to the baptismal action and
event itself:

> So this is what's going on when we pour the baptismal water over
> these unsuspecting, fuzzy little heads:
>
> We are saying to these little ones, "We don't know what life is
> going to bring you. It may be easy, and it may be hard. We pray it will
> be long and happy, but we can't promise. But this we can promise you,
> because God has promised it. We know the end of your story. You
> are loved and claimed—claimed for life, claimed for the future that
> God is working out for human beings and all creation, the future that
> started when Jesus walked out of the tomb as the firstborn of God's
> new creation: unquenchable life.
>
> That's why I say that when we're baptized, we're starting out at
> the end of time.
>
> Because when everything is gone, even time itself, all that will be,
> then, is the open-ended, overflowing, endlessly embracing love and
> mercy and creativity of God, to bless all that we've been, save all that
> got lost, and make us all we're meant to be.
>
> And Charles and Meredith and Laquita?
>
> They'll be there, like all of us, all grown up and yet brand new all
> over again. Because here at the font, God is saying so, here and now.

A Communion Sermon, "Crumbs under the Table,"
by Rev. Cathy Felber

This sermon was preached by Rev. Cathy Felber, a United Methodist
pastor. In contrast to the sermon above, she begins with a text that
seems unrelated to the sacramental occasion, a healing story about

Jesus meeting up with a Syrophoenician woman (Mark 7:24–30). Felber leads us to the Table by an indirect path, a strategy that ultimately produces strikingly fresh insight.

At first, only the occasion on which Felber's sermon is preached—a Communion service—leads us to expect a sacrament-centered sermon. Felber bases her sermon on Mark's account of Jesus's encounter with a Syrophoenician woman who throws herself at his feet, begging for the healing of her demon-possessed daughter.

Felber begins her sermon in an unlikely way: she introduces us to the aging, eight-pound Chihuahua, Rambo, that she and her husband own. Advancing in dog years, Rambo was "old, senile, hard of hearing and almost blind," says Felber, "but he never lost his sense of eat." Of all the eating opportunities Rambo loved, his favorite was "the floor feast." Especially when young relatives—grandchildren, nieces, nephews—came to visit, the "pickin's" on the floor were rich indeed. Admitting that Rambo with his eagerness for "floor food" makes an unlikely start for a sermon, Felber transitions to the biblical story.

Felber takes us on scene by sketching in stream-of-consciousness style the desperate thoughts of the Syrophoenician mother, fretting over her daughter, whose sweat-matted hair and contorted body signal the child's inner torture as a demonic presence assails her. The distressed mother's thoughts are interrupted by brief dialogue with a neighbor who has rushed in to tell her that the Jewish healer, Jesus of Nazareth, has come to their town. The Syrophoenician woman rushes to see Jesus, throwing herself at his feet.

Skillfully, Felber slows the pace, pausing to let us see two sets of tired eyes lock on one another, the "tender" ones of Jesus and the "tear-blurred" ones of the woman as their dialogue unfolds. The woman blurts out her anguished plea that Jesus help her child. But for all his tenderness, Jesus "knows his mission is for the children of Israel . . . not yet for the Gentiles," and so he refuses: "First let the children be fed until they are full. It's not right to take bread from the children and throw it to the dogs."

Two things are worthy of note here. First, Felber does not pursue the implicit slur in this reply (which may be a proverb). While that may well be a sermon worth preaching, that is not the purpose of this one. Second, Felber glosses Jesus's reply somewhat, supplying implicit theological reflection on the possible motivation behind Jesus's reply. Such paraphrasing can serve as theological reflection in the telling of the story, although it must be done judiciously and generally works best in contexts in which most listeners to the sermon are quite familiar with the story as it stands in the received biblical text.

The frantic mother is quick on her feet. She parries: "Sir, even the dogs under the table get to eat the crumbs that fall while the children are eating. The crumbs, sir, I just need the crumbs." Felber's gloss, the added final phrase, is deliberate; she wants us to focus on those crumbs! Jesus affirms her faith and announces that the demon has left her daughter. Felber closes the scene with a glimpse of the Syrophoenician mother's exuberant dash back home.

With deft efficiency, Felber moves us on to a new scene: "In spring 2000, another Gentile woman had a divine appointment with Jesus in another house." She begins with "I quickly slipped into my seat in the seminary chapel," and we know we are hearing her own experience. We learn that on that morning she "was especially troubled and desperate . . . the child in my soul was telling me I didn't belong here; I wasn't smart enough . . . I didn't deserve to be at seminary." Felber gives us just enough information to align her desperation with that of the Syrophoenician woman's, but she is a wise preacher; she does not let her own story take over here. She leaves the details loose enough that we, the listeners, can perhaps identify the "desperate," underqualified scared kid in ourselves.

Felber segues toward the Table: "And then the Communion service began." She evokes the experience by quoting lines from the Communion liturgy being spoken by the student servers, at the head of the aisle, to each worshiper who comes forward. We are listening in—"The body of Christ which was broken for you . . . the blood of Christ which was shed for you."/"The body of Christ which was broken for you . . . the blood of Christ which was shed for you"—when Felber exclaims, "And then I saw them! Why I had never seen them before—on the royal blue carpet, around the servers' feet—I don't know." Felber has not told us *what* she is seeing, but we've already begun to guess as she turns the sermon toward its close: "The words of the prayer came to mind: 'We do not presume to come to this thy table, O merciful Lord, trusting in our own righteousness, but in thy manifold and tender mercies.' The crumbs. I saw the crumbs."

Again quoting the Prayer of Humble Access from Rite I in the Episcopal *Book of Common Prayer*, Felber ties this moment back to the biblical text and presses her sermon's implicit claim that this is about mercy, not qualification: "We are not worthy so much as to gather up the crumbs under thy table. But thou art the same Lord whose property is always to have mercy." Felber concludes:

> Jesus still meets people in the continuity of time and history.
> The usher tells me it's time to get out of my seat. It's time to come to the table. [Jesus] gave me, his child, more than crumbs—just as he had given that other woman.

Felber's sermon demonstrates that, in preaching on the sacraments, we do not always need to use a biblical text that explicitly refers to the Lord's Table or to baptism in some way. Other biblical texts, too, align with the central theological dynamic of the sacraments—that it is God's radical mercy, not our efforts or qualifications, that grounds all our hope.

Preaching about How We Use Power

Nothing will repay preacher and congregation more richly than sermons at regular intervals that foreground the crucial importance of fair, accessible distribution of decision-making power in communities that claim to testify to the love and justice of God. Such sermons not only contribute to the health of a congregation, but also help individual church members hold themselves and others accountable for the fair distribution and use of power. This wisdom can spill over into the decision-making structures in which they participate in their weekday lives.

As noted earlier in this chapter, a congregation or its denominational bodies may have official policies calling for equal distribution of all leadership and decision-making roles, regardless of gender identity, cultural background, or socioeconomic status. Yet a disproportionate exercise of power—on the part of males over females, rich over poor, or the congregation's dominant ethnicity over all minorities in the congregation—often exists in congregations. When this happens, pastoral and lay leaders need to analyze what's going on and investigate the root causes of the imbalance. Is it related to local cultural norms? Congregational history or simple force of habit? Or is the majority (or the most powerful of several minorities) in the congregation wielding undue influence and resisting the theological norms that are meant to govern the congregation's life?

Sadly, in the name of congregational "unity," or of being "nice" or "Christian," leaders too often turn a blind eye to such dynamics. But unity at the price of stifling the voices and insights of a significant number of members, to protect a few brittle egos, is simply too high a price to pay.

Moreover, it is precisely these "unofficial" maldistributions of power in a congregation that most quickly stifle a congregation's worship and witness. It's a mistake to assume that visitors to a congregation will not pick up on dynamics like these. They do. Newcomers can sniff out distortions in the power structure of a congregation better than seasoned members who've been around these dynamics for so long that they've become desensitized to them. Unhealthy power dynamics create an atmosphere of inhospitality.

The courageous preacher, after due deliberation and discernment with lay leadership, will address the subject of fair, humble, accountable uses of power. It is this kind of courageous proclamation that is *most* likely to encourage church members to risk faithfully improvisational, redemptive interruption of business as usual that challenges abuses of power in the wider world.

A Sample Sermon: The Use or Abuse of Power

The Rev. Dr. Susan Cartmell, pastor of Pilgrim Congregational Church (UCC) in Harwich Port, Massachusetts, takes up the well-known story of David and Bathsheba in 2 Samuel 11–12 and examines it, not as an isolated adulterous affair, but as an abuse of power. The impact of this sermon derives partly from its timeliness. Cartmell preached this interpretation of 2 Samuel 11:26–12:10 amid the growing #MeToo movement of 2017–18 (mentioned in the sermon).

| Rev. Susan Cartmell, "What Have You Done?"[7]

Cartmell's sermon begins straightforwardly, with the central character in the events of 2 Samuel 11:26–12:10, the Israelite king, David. Cartmell begins with a quick sketch of David, a figure with admirable qualities for leadership:

> David was a charismatic leader, a brilliant strategist, an ambitious politician, and a man of enormous personal energy. . . . From his childhood when he showed up to do battle with a sling, he was able to assess danger, recognize opportunity, and face fear. Stories of his military escapades dazzle the imagination; and though they may have grown in the telling, no one doubts his prowess.

Cartmell's portrait of David is credible, even to contemporary ears. There is every reason to admire him. Yet, observes Cartmell, "David's . . . ambitious way of taking property extended to women, too."

Cartmell quickly reviews the sequence of events: David strolls on the upper balcony of the palace, he spots Bathsheba bathing on a distant roof, and he summons her—because he can. Noteworthy here is that Cartmell refuses to supply a detail that many a preacher seems to insert—that there was something deliberately seductive in Bathsheba's bathing on the roof, an idea for which there is no evidence. David "forced himself" upon Bathsheba—but some time later Bathsheba sends word she is pregnant.

Cartmell pauses in the tale to underscore some uncomfortable dimensions of this story:

7. Rev. Susan Cartmell, "What Have You Done?," *Day1.org* podcast. Downloaded and transcribed from http://day1.org/8245-susan_cartmell_what_have_you_done.

Now Bathsheba was married, and her husband was a good man, a loyal officer in David's own army, but it didn't matter to David who Bathsheba was married to. It didn't matter how much his rape hurt her or her husband.

Some will object that Cartmell's portrait of David is too harsh; isn't David remembered in the tradition as "a man after God's own heart"? That is true; but Cartmell forestalls any effort on our part to make this situation less heinous by imagining that there was love involved, or by presuming that Bathsheba was flattered by the king's attention, or any other mitigating gloss that we might add to the story to avoid what is starkly obvious: "This is not about passion," warns Cartmell. "It was always about prerogative and power."

Moving on to the prophet Nathan's confrontation with David, Cartmell points out that in the original language, "the Hebrew is spitting out the truth in stark two-word sentences—things that translate, 'I'm pregnant' . . . 'You are the man' . . . 'I have sinned against God.'"

David's story, says Cartmell, "is as old as time," and it is utterly contemporary. This is where Cartmell states what has surely already been on the minds of at least some of her listeners:

Starting last October, a group of actresses, including Gwyneth Paltrow, Ashley Judd, and Rose McGowen, came forward to reveal that they had been sexually molested by Hollywood producer Harvey Weinstein. Their brave testimonies sparked the #MeToo Movement which has revealed an epidemic of harassment and rape.

Cartmell cuts to the heart of the matter: "Whether [in] the board room or [on] the battlefield, abuse thrives where everyone is afraid, where the weak are expendable and where people can take advantage of others without recourse." David's cover-up, she observes, reveals that abuse is typically not an isolated act, but a pattern—"a kind of hubris that grows over time . . . a march down the highway of entitlement." Eventually, "[David] has crossed so many lines he cannot seem to help himself." He sets up his loyal soldier Uriah, Bathsheba's husband, for certain death on the battlefield, and in no time, Bathsheba is a widow.

Cartmell turns again at this point from the biblical text to present realities. Citing in addition to the #MeToo movement the tidal wave of clergy sexual-abuse cases steadily coming to light in the courts, Cartmell puts her finger on the core strategy of abusive power's self-preservation: "a series of decisions to preserve the power of some and promote the abuse of others."

Drawing toward the sermon's close, Cartmell makes the issue of the power we have, and how we use it, personal. She tells how, a few years back, her young granddaughter, who in school had been studying the civil rights movement of the 1960s, asked her a question: "What did you do, Grandma? Did you march with Dr. King?" Cartmell explained to her granddaughter that she was only a fifth grader then and had had to stay in school. But, she says, the question would not leave her:

> What did you do, Grandma, when unarmed Black men and women were routinely shot by police in their cars or at public parks or in their own backyards? Did you write to your Senator? Did you march with them? Did you run for office? What did you do to fight racism? . . . What did you do, Grandma, when you saw a picture . . . of plastic sludge in the ocean . . . the result of 19 billion pounds of garbage dumped in the ocean every year? What did you do . . . ?

Homiletically, the wisdom of this strategy on Cartmell's part is that she does not interrogate the listeners, as many a less experienced preacher might have done. ("What did *you* do?" or "Here is the problem . . . what are *you* doing about it?") Rather, by simply inserting "Grandma," she makes it clear that she too has to answer the questions she has been raising in this sermon about the use of our power. We, her listeners, can readily identify.

Only at the sermon's close does Cartmell turn to us, and she does so with empathy:

> You are not the king of Israel. . . . You have never killed anybody, and you don't intend to . . . you may feel overwhelmed or powerless most days. [Yet] the story of David is a dramatic reminder that we

all have influence. We all make decisions which can change other people's lives.

The sermon's close is brief; nowhere does Cartmell resort to the language of "must," "ought," and "should." Rather, she names some of the roles, gifts, and opportunities that many of us, her listeners, are likely to have—most of it simply by virtue of being born in a fortunate place, in a powerful and rich nation.

"All of it is a gift from God, the Bible says," Cartmell concludes. "And God is watching."

Cartmell's straightforward sermon about power abuse is all the more compelling against the backdrop of events that accompanied it; yet she makes it clear that this is not merely a political or social question, but also a theological one; and its relevance is perennial.

Preaching on Practices of Public Witness

The embodied public practices of Christian communities in the wider world articulate, not simply in words but through embodied action, a vision of human flourishing rooted in the radical mercy, inclusive love, and restorative justice of God. Christian witness—whether at the communal level (as when a congregation undertakes a project to provide winter shelter for its city's homeless) or at the individual level (in acts of mercy, care, and justice-making)—is embodied, not just verbalized.

Two sermons that deal with the church's public witness follow. The first, by a youth member of a congregation situated at the edge of a university campus, connects worship with public witness with striking simplicity, yet remarkable depth. The second, by seasoned preacher and retired seminary administrator Harry Freebairn, gets at the topic of hospitality to strangers (a primary form of Christian public witness since the church's beginnings) by skillfully enlisting his listeners to identify with the outside, the excluded, the "other."

With the instincts of a preacher, youth preacher Nikhil Pulimood, a
recent confirmand in his Presbyterian congregation, starts not with
high-toned religious talk about prayer, but with literal bread—the
kind he likes to eat, he says, by the loaf, without butter, right before
a race. His listeners' attention now captured with this vivid, multi-
sensory beginning move, Pulimood goes on to say that the bread
we pray for is not just physical, but also *spiritual*. "The bread that we
ask for is greater than any tangible gift we could seek. It's the Bread
of Life, the Living Bread, the stuff that gives life to the world" (39).

In the second paragraph of his sermon, Pulimood raises the
central question that drives his sermon and proposes the answer
he hopes to demonstrate:

> So where does that bread come from? We can rule out Panera,[9] and
> God hasn't been raining down manna for a few years. The source
> of the bread is found in our very appeal: "*Give us this day our daily
> bread.*" . . . Jesus' words . . . are directed to God but are a call to each
> of us. (39)

Jesus himself, says Pulimood, shows us what it looks like to give the
bread that people need, spiritual and literal. Jesus sought time alone
with his disciples after the death of his cousin John, says Pulimood,
but the crowd got wind of his itinerary and got to the deserted place
ahead of him. But Jesus gives them what they most need: the words
that are Bread of Life, and then "to top it all off he performed his
greatest miracle, the one recorded in all four gospels, the big kahuna
for these people whom he sees as his sisters and brothers in need" (40).

8. Nikhil Pulimood, "Youth Sunday Sermon," in *Lord, Teach Us to Pray: Sermons on the Lord's Prayer*, ed. David A. Davis (Princeton, NJ: Clear Faith, 2015),
39–41. In the paragraphs that follow, page references from this sermon are given
in parentheses in the text.

9. A local franchise of this well-known restaurant chain, famous for its bread,
is located a block from Nassau Presbyterian Church, Princeton, New Jersey, where
this sermon was preached.

Now, Pulimood brings things close to home, focusing his listeners on those in need near at hand: a fellow high school student, who—thanks to one bad decision—was arrested and will live with this on his record. A wrongfully imprisoned man, befriended by the congregation—cleared of charges, but then reincarcerated due to a technicality.

"From where does the bread come for those incarcerated among the largest prison population in the world?" asks Pulimood. "Where do the many other casualties of the criminal justice system seek for spiritual, mental, and physical sustenance?" The answer lies in our very petition that God would fill these needs—the "us" in the petition for daily bread. "The collective us, the children of God, the sinners and saints" are the means by which God answers the prayer.

Pulimood closes with the declaration that "the prayer is not so much a grocery list offered up to the Almighty but . . . a collective affirmation, a unified pronouncement that as children of God we . . . accept our roles as deliverers of the Bread of Life, the Living Bread, the stuff that gives life to the world given us by God" (41).

Pulimood's sermon, with its double "take" on bread, refuses to separate bread for the body from bread for the soul or prioritize one over the other. Both matter. Jesus shows us we can't give one without attending to the other. We implicate ourselves in this bread distribution, every time we pray the Lord's Prayer. The effect of Pulimood's sermon, of course, is to reveal that the practices of Christian communities are not pick and choose; they are deeply intertwined. Our practices of praying for daily bread and giving to meet human need, physical and spiritual, are bound inseparably together. Our bread prayer—the Lord's Prayer—points us toward the doors, into the street, and into places like prisons, where human hungers run sharp and deep for the Bread that satisfies.

| HARRY FREEBAIRN, "GOT A DATE WITH AN ANGEL"[10]

Freebairn's sermon on the practice of hospitality is twenty years old, but its subject matter could not be more timely as we near the third decade of the twenty-first century. Never has the sense that

10. Harry Freebairn, "Got a Date with an Angel," *Journal for Preachers* 20, no. 1

the one who is different, who is "other," is a threat to our safety and to our way of life been more palpable in North American society than it is now. Freebairn takes a topical approach, gleaning the wisdom of several biblical texts, including Genesis 18 (where two strangers who seem not quite of this world visit Abraham and Sarah and promise a child), Ephesians 2 (where we learn that we are all strangers, away from "home"), and Hebrews 13:2 (notice that the hospitable may "entertain angels without knowing it").

Freebairn, often something of a jokester, begins his sermon with a story about the shopkeeper who, in keeping with the admonition in Matthew 25 to "take in" the stranger, quite *literally* "takes a stranger in"—selling a cheap blanket for an outrageous price to an unsuspecting out-of-towner. But Freebairn's light-hearted story forms a segue to serious talk: talk about the suspicion we so often harbor against strangers, which sometimes makes us feel entitled to treating them with hostility (18).

Freebairn describes his own sense of disorientation and, at times, near desperation, as a "stranger" after first moving to Princeton. Used to life in a small city in Pennsylvania where he'd lived for years, Freebairn describes his sense of being held under suspicion until proven safe. Recalling what it was like to move through social events where nearly everyone there was a stranger to him, Freebairn confesses, "You feel like a pest if you recognize anyone, because you latch onto those people like a leech, and you do not care" (19).

This move is skillful; instead of trying to persuade us to be hospitable, Freebairn invites his listeners to identify what it feels like to *be* the stranger, the one under suspicion. This becomes Freebairn's segue to his Scripture texts. Ephesians reminds us that "as God's people we are strangers, all of us, who are on the journey together through this dangerous world." And, "if we are strangers by definition, then we know how to recognize other strangers . . . we know what strangers need to feel at home" (19).

Genesis 18 shows the possibility that the stranger may be not a threat, but the bearer of gifts; but we'll never discover that unless

---

(1996): 18–21. In the paragraphs that follow, page references from this article are given in parentheses in the text.

we let go of "our sense that we must protect ourselves and build fortresses against the stranger."

Freebairn tells a story from author Sue Monk Kidd, who was forced along with the rest of the youth group to visit a nursing home and distribute crepe-paper bouquets. When it came time to deliver hers, Kidd threw her bouquet into the lap of an old woman. Before she could leave, the woman spoke: "You didn't want to come, did you, child?" When Kidd protested that sure, of course she did, the old woman, knowing that wasn't true, said, "You can't force the heart." In that woman, by whom her heart was "pushed toward the new direction of compassion," Kidd felt she'd encountered the unexpected "angel" of whom Hebrews speaks (20–21).

Freebairn's sermon closes with lines as fresh today as they were twenty years ago, both enlarging the challenge of hospitality to the global scale and bringing it home to the seminary community he is addressing:

> As churches burn because racial lines refuse to be blurred; as news from military bases causes all of us to be ashamed; as violence becomes the heritage of children in cities and quiet communities like this one, the call to hospitality takes on renewed urgency. It cannot happen out there if it does not happen here. Here, the insider and the outsider have gifts to offer one another, if only we follow Christ's invitation to listen and reach out and meet Him in one another. (21)

A wise and experienced preacher, Freebairn does not close with a ringing series of imperatives about what we "ought to do" and "must do" if the world is ever going to change; rather, he issues an invitation to risk hospitality to whoever is, for us, the "outsider," for that is our best chance in this world of meeting Christ.

Christian Practices as the Claim of God's Future on Our (Material) Lives

As we argued in chapter 3, the "end" or horizon of Christian hope is established in the resurrection of Jesus Christ as the firstborn of God's new creation. The end to which all of our practices point, and from which they take their coherence, is that renewed creation that God has established with the resurrection of Jesus Christ, the firstborn of the future that awaits (Isa. 43:18–19 and 65:17–25; 2 Cor. 5:17; Col. 1:18–20; and Rev. 21:1–5).

God's promised renewal of all things in mercy and justice exerts a redemptive tension, drawing us toward this horizon, even as we are invested, day to day, in the concerns of the present. In our practices, we experience in embodied ways the "pull" of God's redemptive future on our imperfect relationships and our material lives.

We need these practices, because the magnetic pull of short-term reward systems that promise a bracing shot of abundance or an exhilarating surge of feeling powerful is strong. Yet if we let mindful engagement in Christian practices of worship, formation, care, and witness shape us, we have a good, God-given chance of staying alert to God's presence and activity found in unlikely places in everyday life, far from the glitz, the glamour, and the power plays. All Christian practices aim to "rehearse" us, amid the imperfections and struggle of our present experience, for the wholeness of life for which we are made, and to which we are called.

Further Reading:
Practice-Centered Thought in Theology and Preaching

Theologians—especially practical theologians—have taken up practice theory into their work in varied ways. Readers are encouraged to think carefully, reading these works, about the degree to which varied cultural influences shape all human practices, including the ways we read Scripture. Contextualized preaching on practices is essential in forming the courageous, faithfully improvisational witness of Christians in everyday life.

Bass, Dorothy C. *Practicing Faith: A Way of Life for a Searching People.* San Francisco: Jossey-Bass, 2010.

————, and Susan R. Briehl. *On Our Way: Christian Practices for Living a Whole Life.* Nashville: Upper Room, 2010.

Dykstra, Craig R. *Growing in the Life of Faith: Education and Christian Practices.* Louisville: Geneva, 1999.

Schlafer, David J., and Timothy F. Sedgwick. *Preaching What We Practice: Proclamation and Moral Discernment.* Harrisburg, PA: Morehouse, 2007.

Tanner, Kathryn. *Theories of Culture: A New Agenda for Theology.* Minneapolis: Fortress, 1997.

CHAPTER 5

Story as Rehearsal Space: Preaching the Dynamics of Hope-Driven Action

Stories are part of the repertoire of virtually every Christian preacher. Two primary reasons for this is are obvious. First, narrative material is prominent in the church's Scriptures. As we noted in chapter 1, it is debatable whether we can honor the full complexity of the Christian canon by reading it as a single, unbroken storyline; yet much canonical material has been passed on to us in the form of stories.

Second, even if a preacher's storytelling skills are limited, most listeners will tune in when she or he begins, "I heard a story about two brothers . . ." or "Maybe you saw that story in the newspaper about . . ." Why is it that heads come up and listeners focus when a story begins? One reason is that we think, and even dream, in stories. It is by story that we seem to make sense of our own lives and understand other lives. We are constantly revising our interpretations of the world, and our own role in it, past and present, through the stories that we hear and tell.

The Role of Stories in Building Self-Understanding and Christian Identity

In his classic 1971 article, "The Narrative Quality of Experience," Stephen Crites argues that "the formal quality of experience through time is inherently narrative."[1] Crites goes on to note that, as chil-

---

1. Stephen Crites, "The Narrative Quality of Experience," in *Why Narrative?*

dren, we gain a sense of who we are and where we have come from through the stories our parents and others tell us.

The stories we hear apprentice us in the art of composing stories. A very young child can put together the rudiments of a story almost as soon as she or he can acquire enough vocabulary, even if some narrative ingredients are missing. At first, a small child tends to recite a series of events, real or imagined, in a rush of loosely connected subject/verb or subject/verb/direct object sentences—something like, "the dog ran and it was raining . . . the cat said 'meow!' . . . but the boy wasn't, because he was eating peanut butter." We are a little short on dramatic tension and denouement here, but it is a start. Our skills steadily improve, and our sense of being a separate self is partly established by the way we choose to tell our stories, connecting one episode with others.

In other words, our sense of ourselves within the world, at first dependent on cues and responses from our immediate caregivers, becomes more and more (as we grow up) the product of our inner "narration" of past experiences. As life experience unfolds, we subtly edit our self-descriptive narratives, incorporating new insights and accenting different things. New experience causes us, in retrospect, to understand ourselves differently. But thinking "narratively" doesn't only help us make sense of our past; a sense of narrative coherence also enables us to anticipate our future path and its consequences.

There is a photo in our family album where my nearly two-year-old self has seized a good-sized shock of my three-year-old brother's thick blonde hair. It's easy to see that I am yanking upward with energy, concentration, and just a touch of smugness. My gleeful expression in the photo gives me away: clearly, I had anticipated with some satisfaction my brother's open-mouthed howl of pained outrage. Our ability to size up our opportunities for agency falls into place early.

Readings in Narrative Theology, ed. Stanley Hauerwas and L. Gregory Jones (Grand Rapids: Eerdmans, 1989), 66; essay originally published as "The Narrative Quality of Experience," *Journal of the American Academy of Religion* 39, no. 3 (1971): 291–311. Many of my observations in this section depend, directly or indirectly, or Crites's insights into the narrative quality of human self-consciousness.

In fact, posits Paul Ricoeur, through inner narration, we anticipate for ourselves a course of action—sometimes in a matter of microseconds—in an immediate setting. We're capable of sizing up very quickly the demands and opportunities a situation presents. This, as we learned in chapter 3, is what Ricoeur calls "imaginative rehearsal." A similar, but slowed-down, form of imaginative rehearsal was playing out the other day one table away from me in the seminary cafeteria. A group of seminary friends were working out plans for their Friday night. Possible scenarios were proposed, amended, withdrawn, and replaced with new proposals. Anticipated obstacles to agency (capacity to act) were up for debate: "There are seven of us, but we only have one working car." Thumbs tapped cell-phone screens. "We could walk to the movie, but we'd've had to start ten minutes ago to catch the 5:30 showing," someone said, still focused on the screen. "Wait!" one of them interjected. "Andy's sitting right over there, and he borrowed my car last week; he owes me one!" New possible storylines suddenly came into play.

Thinking narratively, we project and test possible courses of action. We use imagination to experiment with possible paths of agency (capacity to act) in given settings and circumstances. The setting of anticipated action entails both opportunities and constraints that bear on the possible plots (courses of action) that can unfold. Stories in sermons can be thought of as shared experiments—shared imaginative rehearsal for the possibilities for action in settings that preacher and congregation alike recognize.

Sermons that make generous use of narrative are usually of two types. First, there are sermons in which the underlying biblical text, or texts, become the storied "space" that preacher and congregation "inhabit" together, imaginatively. Along the way, the preacher will draw analogies with contemporary experience. In other sermons, the narrative material is drawn primarily from history, literature or film, or from contemporary experience. This narrative material is aligned, strategically, with narrative or nonnarrative biblical texts, and in the lively space created by this alignment of Scripture and the world of experience, new possibilities for action on our part, in light of God's promises and action in the world, come to light.

In both cases, the aim of the sermon, ultimately, is to imaginatively rehearse courses of action that might realistically play out in the everyday settings of the world our listeners will face on Monday and beyond. Story-driven sermons, like all sermons, operate within the framework of Scripture's testimony to the promise-making, promise-keeping nature of God. We explore biblical stories, stories drawn from history, popular culture, and literature as a way of seeking the possibilities for living with agile, imaginative faithfulness amid the specific circumstances and settings of our own particular lives.

To be clear, the aim of this chapter is *not* to provide a complete introduction to what is known as *narrative* preaching. The term *narrative preaching*, frequently misunderstood to refer to *any* sermon that includes storytelling, is actually a specific approach to sermon design in which the logic of the sermon unfolds according to the problem/complication/situation-changing clue/resolution pattern common to stories. Many good introductions to narrative preaching exist, particularly the work of narrative homiletician Eugene Lowry.[2]

Sermons constructed according to the *logic* of narrative, described above, often *do* follow storylines, biblical and contemporary, since these are a natural fit for narrative sermon design. Yet narratively structured sermons can employ nonnarrative materials, as well. For example, the situation-shifting "clue" in a narrative-type sermon could, conceivably, take the form of a theological insight drawn from a biblical text, creed, or hymn.

In some preaching traditions, stories play the fairly limited role of serving strictly as "illustrations" to put flesh on the bones of an outline made up of ideas or concepts derived from a biblical text. (Surprisingly, in some such traditions, biblical stories are not allowed

2. See, for example, Eugene Lowry, *The Sermon: Dancing the Edge of Mystery* (Nashville: Abingdon, 1997); and Lowry, *How to Preach a Parable: Designs for Narrative Sermons* (Nashville: Abingdon, 1989). Lowry's career as a homiletician has been devoted to developing ways that narrative structure can inform sermon design, allowing listeners to experience the gospel as an event of transformation rather than as mere information.

to speak for themselves *as* stories; they, too, are reduced to a list of moral precepts or doctrinal concepts!) What I am advocating in this chapter is a range of uses of stories—biblical, historical, and contemporary—that allow them to become spaces of *imaginative rehearsal* for those in the pews. I do not advocate reducing stories, biblical or otherwise, to a set of propositions or moral admonitions at the end of the sermon so as to make them "applicable." Stories have been handed to us by the tradition *as* narrative material for a reason: narratives with which we can identify prod us into active reflection about human experience generally, and our own in particular. Only a few biblical stories end with a moral exhortation. The story of the rich fool (Luke 12:13–21), with its tagline ending ("This is how it will be with whoever stores up things for themselves, but is not rich toward God," v. 21, New International Version), might be cited as an example. But even here, the tagline takes shape as a posited action, not a "must," "ought," or "should" statement. We must still explore what that action might look like and where it might lead.

Stories can function as powerful prompts to creative action *without* being attached to (or worse, reduced to!) a series of propositions. While stories *can* be used to illustrate or amplify ideas in a sermon whose core structure is made up of conceptual points, a well-illustrated argument is by no means the only means of persuasion in the preacher's tool kit. Preachers who manage stories skillfully proceed from the assumption that, if a story is skillfully told, listeners can compare the setting and situation of a story (biblical or otherwise) to their own settings and situations and, in so doing, "rehearse" possible courses of action in those everyday settings. Truth be told, inviting listeners into the dynamics of a narrative's world can work as powerfully as, if not *more* powerfully than, a series of principles at the sermon's close meant to instigate courageously faithful action on the part of our listeners when they step into the Monday world.

Ideally, the aim of story-driven preaching is *to transfer the work of imagination from the preacher to the listener*. I advocate inviting our listeners to step *inside* stories and *explore* them from the inside out, instead of explaining stories so as to reduce them to a set of moral instructions. We can explore a story either from the point of view of characters in the story or by observing the unfolding action of the story at close range.

How Narrative Material Creates Spaces
of Imaginative Rehearsal

Whatever the story we are telling, our aim is to project on the screen of our listeners' imaginations a particular kind of world (setting and situation), seen from a perspective that invites our listeners' identification with the unfolding action. To invite listeners into the space of a story—to put them "on scene," if you will—we need to show listeners where they are, who's there with them, what has happened or is about to happen to them, and what's at stake for us as the action unfolds. (What in the situation is problematic? What is complicating the situation? What do we hope for?)

Good pulpit storytellers may "wonder aloud" about the motivation for characters' action, but they do not *determine and explain* those motivations, unless that detail is already in the story itself. For example, nowhere does the story of the prodigal son explain (a) why the prodigal wants to take his share of the inheritance and take off; (b) why the father races out to meet his wastrel son when he spots him "a long way off"; or (c) precisely why the elder brother is so disdainful and angry about the lavish celebration of his brother's return (at least not fully, although we get hints).

If our intent is to give space for listeners *themselves* to test the elements of the story and ponder the motivations of its characters for their actions and reactions, we need to invite them to identify, or empathize, with a particular character or point of view. A listener will need to identify with (or, entering imaginatively into the story's space, "stand alongside") a particular character to explore specific possibilities for action that the setting and circumstances of the story affords. Good storytelling preachers don't ask their listeners to identify with every point of view at once. Asking listeners to imaginatively race around a complex story and experience it from every available point of view can be exhausting for the listeners and ultimately less productive. When there is more than one point of view available in a story, biblical or otherwise (and there usually is), the one with which we invite listeners to identify depends on our knowledge of our listeners themselves and the sorts of questions the story might raise for them.

For example, recently I assigned some of my beginning students Luke 13:10–17, the story of Jesus's liberating healing of the bent-over woman, as a preaching text. Some students adopted the point of view of the bent-over woman herself. Others took the perspective of the amazed onlookers. But others invited us to identify with the synagogue ruler. We were, after all, seminarians or trained preacher-homileticians. Certainly we were the kinds of folk who have a pretty deep investment in making worship unfold as it should. In other words, we comprised an audience who had all kinds of reasons to empathize with the concerns of the character in the story who is trying to sort out what should happen on the Sabbath and what needs to happen on other days of the week. This point of view made for some particularly thought-provoking preaching.

Unfortunately, some preachers do tell stories but then feel obligated to tell their listeners what each character "must" be feeling, or manage their listeners' reactions to the story frame by frame, as if to make sure they make the "right" sense of the story. This kind of overbearing management of imagination in the pulpit undermines the power of the narrative to draw us into active investment in the questions it raises and the constraints and opportunities for action that it poses. Short-circuiting listeners' engagement with a story deprives them of the process of imaginative rehearsal that is so essential to generating creative action.

At first, some preachers are reluctant to "trust" their listeners with a story. But once a group of students or working preachers has experimented with inviting listeners into a story, without managing their reactions to it, their trust in the process deepens. Preachers begin to recognize the power of *not* overexplaining, assigning inner thoughts to every character, or prompting their listeners on how to feel. To summarize, it isn't our job to "explain" stories, but to allow our listeners to experience them as *spaces of imaginative rehearsal for action in the world.* Toward the end of this chapter, we will explore three sermons that, in different ways, manage narrative material well.

The Types of Stories Our Listeners Need to Hear

Before turning to sermon examples, we'll briefly consider in this section three types of stories that have something essential to contribute to our listeners' capacity for the kind of imaginative rehearsal that leads to faithful, improvisational action in their everyday world.

First, and perhaps most obvious, will be biblical stories. As we have argued in part I, discovering and undertaking faithful courses of action in everyday settings can be thought of as analogous to a classical jazz musician's reinterpretation of familiar tunes and harmonies of the deep tradition of jazz for a particular performance moment and setting. Such reinterpretation is possible only when there is a deep well of memory and familiarity with that tradition on which to draw. Similarly, individual Christians need to *know* the tradition before they can *draw upon* that tradition. The stories of the Bible are an essential part of that deep traditioning.

Second, we'll consider the role of stories from Christian histories (tapping into traditions beyond our own), and third, we'll explore the use of contemporary stories to which our listeners can relate, and how best to choose these.

Stories from the Bible Itself

Narrative material is the genre of biblical literature with which most readers of the Bible are most familiar. Stories form vast portions of the canonical Scriptures of Hebrew Scripture and the New Testament. Knowing biblical stories well enough to recall them and test their relevance to our own situation is part of becoming a faithfully improvisational witness to the ways of God in our own time and place.

I argued in the previous chapter that the deep "heartbeat," or recurring motif, that links together the diverse literary genres of the Christian canon is divine promise. We can find this promise motif embedded in all kinds of literature, from wisdom books like Psalms and Proverbs to the oracles of the prophets and the apocalyptic vision of John in the book of Revelation. But the portrayal of God as maker and keeper of life- and world-changing promises is most prominent in the narratives we find throughout the Hebrew Scriptures and New Testament.

Many twenty-first-century preachers are rediscovering how crucial it is to spend time telling and exploring the stories of the Bible. An occupational hazard of preachers is to assume too readily that somehow those in our pews have picked up the same familiarity with the Bible's stories and the resonances between its major storylines that *we* picked up in seminary. This is far from true. More and more in the pews know less and less of what is in the Bible. Their exposure might come from a high school literature course where they read parts of the Bible as classic literature. Some have picked up their knowledge from movies, television specials, or the internet.

This lack of familiarity means that twenty-first-century preachers need to devote time to simply orienting their congregations to the basic narrative "backbone" of the Christian canon. As these stories become familiar, those in the pews will begin to sense the narrative arc of the canon, presenting God not only as the creator of life, but as dedicated divine agent of creation's reclamation and restoration.

At the core of the biblical story, for Christians, are the four Gospels. In different ways, they narrate the life, ministry, death, and resurrection of Jesus. Preachers who follow the cycles of the Revised Common Lectionary find themselves returning again and again to the birth and passion narratives, as well as miracle stories and parables. But these stories are best understood when our listeners can relate them to the Old Testament backdrop on which the Gospels depend and to which they often allude.

The Old Testament, no less than the New, presents the God of Israel as a God of covenant, a maker and keeper of promises. The stories of the patriarchs (Abraham, Isaac, and Jacob), the story of Moses and the Exodus, and the stories of prominent kings, like David and Saul, as well as judges, like Samuel, Deborah, and Gideon, and prophets, like Elijah and Elisha, are all referenced in New Testament writings. Key women of the Old Testament are also rich subjects for preaching. Sarah, Rachel, and Rebekah; Miriam and Rahab; Ruth, Hannah, and Esther all play distinctive roles in the story of the ethnic, cultural, and religious traditions that shaped Jesus's life, and some are named as Jesus's ancestors in the genealogies of Matthew and Luke.

In the New Testament, the story of the church's Spirit-driven beginnings, including the missions of Peter, Paul, and others, sheds light on the dynamics of Christian witness in the cosmopolitan world of the Roman Empire. Briefly locating major biblical figures and storylines within the broad sweep of the Bible's overarching sequence of events can be a help to sermon listeners, not only newcomers to faith but the seasoned churchgoer, as well.

An orientation of promise-grounded hope for the future catches up both the stories of the biblical past and our lived present in a single trajectory of openness and possibility—not empty, existential possibility, but the rich possibilities for human flourishing implied by a future birthed out of God's compassion, mercy, and justice. Our hope is not hope for the sake of hope; it is hope in a God whose character we come to know precisely through biblical story. The stories of the Bible matter, even if only for that reason alone. These stories reveal human encounters with the God whose promises reframed *their* experience and, today, reframe *ours*.

We, no less than the fumbling and fallible characters of the Bible, find ourselves in relationship with a God whose promises ignite hope on the horizon of the human future amid the darkest of times. Familiarity with the stories of people of the Bible who struggled to trust divine promises amid disconcerting circumstances and doubt helps us better understand our own struggle to live in the light of divine promise in a world that is more likely to lodge its faith in the stock market, durable goods, guns, and bombs. Reading the stories of faithful people of the past, we learn as they did that living in light of a God-crafted future requires much of us—not only trust, but a willingness to believe that human fulfillment means something other than amassing a disproportionate share of goods, power, and admiration.

Yet the most important feature of biblical stories may be not the realism with which they portray human experience, but what they indicate about the perduring redemptive intentions of God, enacted on the human stage. Biblical stories portray divine character and agency not within some realm of heroes and beasts suspended between earth and heaven, but within the framework of ordinary human life. They testify to a love affair of God with the world God has created, suffered over and suffered for, and intends to rescue from its self-destructive love affair with self-aggrandizement in all forms. Biblical stories portray God as attuned to the cries of the vulnerable, the voiceless, and the despised. These God hears and vindicates—Hagar and Ishmael, Leah, Joseph, the Israelite slaves, Tamar, and many others.

Biblical stories draw us into their world; the preacher's job is to return us to our own with shifted perception. The stories of the canon propose a world that assumes the presence and activity of God. They are dynamic models of human action that sometimes responds to, and other times seems indifferent to, divine presence, intention, and agency (action) in the world. Some biblical stories present exemplary patterns of human action that assume and respond to the presence, intentions, and agency of God in the world, but, of course, many do not.

At times, the storied world of Scripture is as multidimensional and ambiguous as everyday reality itself. Yet, for all this variety and ambiguity, what holds together the many storylines of the canon is a recurring narrative thread of divine redemptive action toward recalcitrant, impetuous, and highly vulnerable human beings. Biblical stories present God interacting with human beings to put in check the human tendency to heedless, heartless self-promotion and, instead, to open paths that lead to sustaining and sustainable communities and practices. Biblical stories, in all their variety, are, for improvisational faithfulness, analogous to the classic melodies and harmonies, including blues-based melodies, that furnish the imaginative repertoire of jazz musicians in the classic tradition. We do not invent faithful patterns of action out of nothing; we stand in a living tradition of faithful improvisation.

Further, as we saw in chapter 3, biblical stories draw us into a world in which human beings have to do with a divine maker and keeper of gracious promises. Among the promises carried by these biblical narratives are promises that stand open ended. We are returned to our world seeing it freshly, within the arc of expectation that the promises of the biblical tradition create, reframed by the open-ended horizon of God's future. A crucial storytelling skill in preaching is to sketch, concretely, what familiar, challenging situations might look like, reimagined within this arc of divine redemptive promise. Such active reimagination in sermons models the imaginative freedom we hope our listeners will dare to embrace, seeing their Monday-to-Saturday world as a landscape in which God is already at work.

Stories from the Christian Past

Wise preachers do not limit themselves to biblical stories alone. We are heirs to a living tradition of improvisational faithfulness on the part of the women and men, the old and the young, who have sought to live faithfully in an array of circumstances—often very trying circumstances—in the past. This wealth of narrative history is underused, in my opinion, in contemporary preaching, and its neglect has significant implications. It is like throwing away all the pictures in the family album; we forget that to get here—gathered at this time, in this place, as a community of faith that does things a particular way—we had to come *from* somewhere (and actually, given the diverse membership of most churches, from many places).

It has often been said that if we forget our past, we are bound to repeat it; and that is certainly true in the church. I find that many church members (and seminary students, for that matter) lack a historical sensibility about theology, church leadership, the practices of worship, and the church's public witness. It is as if one of two things must be true: (a) this (the way we do things or say things) is the way it's always been done or said, and, therefore, it should not be changed; or (b) somebody just made this up a decade or so ago, and throwing it out won't make any difference.

Nothing develops a sense of humility or nudges a congregation toward a bit more generosity of spirit toward each other and toward other expressions of Christianity like a dose of history—or, to put that better, *histories*. The plural is preferable. Gone are the days when we can naively talk about *the* history of *the* church. Multiple histories of multiple churches are out there to be discovered—a rich resource for exploring the connections between the way Christians have believed and worshiped, the way their faith has come to expression in public witness.

Increasingly, we can investigate these multiple histories by deliberately seeking out "unofficial" perspectives and stories told in the voices of those once invisible and silent. Research is expanding to bring to light more and more hidden histories of women and the enslaved in churches within and beyond North America. These alternative interpretations of Christian experience through the centuries allow us to discover surprising exemplars and to see our own experience as but one thread in a vast weave of histories and stories.

There are different historical views of the Roman Catholic churches of the west, with their distinctive cultural settings, versus the eastern, Orthodox traditions—also multiple and diverse. Then there is the whole array of Protestant communions, thriving to greater or lesser degree in cultures around the globe. These many histories are a goldmine of stories, although gaining access to them takes patient prowling through theological libraries and even more patient reading.

The web is also a possible source; but there, publications are often not juried or vetted, and one has to check and recheck information to make sure what one is sharing from the pulpit is accurate and balanced.

Contemporary Stories from Experience, Literature, and Electronic Media

Contemporary stories, too, play an indispensable role in sermons, whether drawn from film, literature, the day's news, or common human experience. Storylines from the world of literature or film can provide compelling, truth-bearing portrayals of life as we experience it, filled with challenging complexity as well as surprising irruptions of grace.

Contemporary stories need to be chosen with care. First, it is crucial that stories be easy to envision and not overly complex. Say, for example, that you wish to relate a moving, tension-filled scene from a film. If, as you rehearse what you will need to do to provide enough setup for listeners to understand the situation, you find yourself trying to explain the interrelationships of six different characters in the film, you will need to set aside this film scene. It's simply too difficult to make it accessible to your listeners.

Second, be careful that a story you tell connects well with your specific listeners. If you are preaching to a congregation that mostly works for hourly wages or lives on social security and relies on food stamps, a story about a dilemma faced by a Wall Street broker is as thoughtless as it is pointless.

Third, if you wish to lay a biblical story alongside a contemporary one, make sure that the inner dynamics of the two stories line up. For example, maybe you've decided to preach on the story of Naaman, the leprous Syrian general. You want to concentrate on the scene in which his wife's unnamed Israelite slave girl suggests that Naaman go to the Israelite prophet, Elisha, to seek healing. On the web, you've stumbled over a story about a young junior-high-school basketball player in Boston, slumped into his seat on the subway headed home, duffle bag on his lap. Shoulders drooping, he's staring at his scuffed basketball shoes, thinking about that flubbed final shot that cost the team the game. He hears someone speaking to him, looks up, and there is one of his professional basketball heroes, standing in front of him. "Tough game?" says the star. "We have those. Don't give up." It's a nice story; the trouble is that it does not line up, in terms of the dynamics between the characters, with the scene between Naaman and the Israelite slave girl. In the Naaman story, the weak and nameless one speaks truth to power; in the web story, the powerful speaks an encouraging word to the weak. The two stories' dynamics collide and confuse the listener.

Contemporary stories come from many sources; and, as we've indicated, often it is single scenes, not entire plotlines, that serve us best in the pulpit. Stories from literature (novels, short stories, and drama) can be useful, if they can be conveyed simply. Also, if we make a habit of reading widely, particularly reading novels and stories about people from other cultures, the stories we tell can broaden our understanding of human life before God in the world and enlarge our own view of the world, as well as that of listeners.[3]

A perennial point of debate among preachers is whether one should use stories from one's own experience. My answer is: sometimes, and judiciously. In telling stories from my own experience, I am asking my listeners to identify with me. That may or may not always be the most useful way to help those in the pew engage in imaginative rehearsal for faithfully improvisational witness in the world of *their* experience. A minister's experience of Christian faith can be quite different from that of those in the pews.

News stories are particularly useful—for several reasons. First, the format of news reporting is such that scenes are already pared to essentials. Second, these are stories already embedded in the common world and experience of listeners. To use news stories, of course, responsible preachers need to do some cross-checking to make sure that the reporting they are accessing is fair, balanced, and accurate. At times, contrasting tellings of a single incident can, in and of themselves, create provocative spaces for examining what sorts of issues are truly at stake in the Monday-to-Saturday world of listeners.

Stories from "sermon-source" sites on the web have to be regarded with particular caution. Sometimes, these stories are overly simple or moralistic, to the point of being implausible. Stories that do not convey the complexity and ambiguity of everyday life are seldom very helpful as imaginative resources for Christians struggling to bear witness to the mercy and justice of God amid the complexities of the workplace or classroom, where many cultures and religious perspectives are represented and one's range of agency (power to act) may be limited.

---

3. Cornelius J. Plantinga recommends wide reading as a basic discipline for all preachers. He provides guidance for choosing what to read, how to read, and how to draw upon one's reading to enrich our preaching (*Reading for Preaching: The Preacher in Conversation with Storytellers, Biographers, Poets, and Journalists* [Grand Rapids: Eerdmans, 2013]).

Sample Sermons: Stories as Spaces
of Imaginative Rehearsal for Faithful Action

Here we will consider three different sermons that explore biblical narratives "from the inside"—making us close observers of the action. First, a sermon by Rev. Sarah Speed McTyre takes us inside the world of the formerly blind man and his critics (John 9), foregrounding the outsider status of Jesus and those he touches and calls. Second, a sermon by Rev. Claudette Copeland steadily interweaves the ongoing experiences of violence and abuse that have marked the lives of hundreds of African American women over many decades with the story of the rape of Tamar by her brother, Amnon (2 Sam. 13:1–22). Finally, we'll explore a sermon by Dean Jacquelyn Lapsley of Princeton Seminary, in which she aligns her seminary audience's contemporary experience with Gideon's encounter—in the winepress where he is threshing wheat—with a divine messenger (Judg. 6:11–15). Readers may also want to return to chapter 2 where we discussed two sermons that foreground tactics of the weak. These sermons make excellent use of narrative material to underscore the difference the simple actions of unlikely agents can make when the well-being of society's most vulnerable is at stake.

Sermon Strategy I: Explore a Biblical Story—
from inside the Action

> Sarah Speed McTyre, "The Formerly Blind Man
> (As If the World Had Not Changed)"[4]

Sarah Speed McTyre begins her sermon on the ninth chapter of John by wondering aloud why the gospel writer felt it necessary to spend a full forty-one verses on a healing he could have reported far more briefly: "Couldn't he have shared this story without drag-

---

4. Sarah Speed McTyre, "The Formerly Blind Man (As If the World Had Not Changed)," *Pulpit Digest* 81, no. 2 (2000): 97–102. In the paragraphs that follow, page references from this sermon are given in parentheses in the text.

ging in the disciples, hauling the man back and forth before the Pharisees, calling in his parents, and even listening to what the neighbors have to say?" Hooking the story deftly to the world of her listeners, McTyre considers how the story of a synagogue-shunned poor fellow might be "beat to death" on the evening newscast, as so many stories of human pathos are. McTyre imagines the earnest neighbor lamenting into the camera how "it really is a shame they had to drive him out of the synagogue in the end . . . such a nice, quiet boy . . . with his disability and all" (97).

McTyre prepares her listeners for the path she will take through this story by observing that the conundrum that continues through forty-one verses does not turn out to be the wonder of blind eyes made to see, but "What do you do with a formerly blind man?" The man has become a problem: "He is not blind anymore, but nobody has any other way to identify and categorize him. . . . Nowhere is he given a name. He is the blind man" (98).

In the wake of such an astonishing change, "you would think the whole gang would turn out and celebrate. Hey, kill the fatted calf! Let the wine flow! . . . The blind guy—well, he isn't anymore!" Note that here, McTyre shifts to first person dialogue set *inside* the space of an imagined scene within the story. With a storyteller's instinct for the power of the particular, she imagines "children bringing him odd things like grasshoppers and worms so he can see them . . . his father awkwardly grabbing him around the shoulders with a catch in his voice: 'How 'bout that—huh? How 'bout that?'" (99).

But, despite the fact that, like creation itself, Jesus has made from mud a new life for this man, "there is no emotional outpouring, no party" here. Instead, "you get the feeling that they wish Jesus hadn't messed with the dirt in their town." The man is a problem. "He can't very well beg anymore. What do the neighbors do when they can no longer see him as less, punished, more sinful, a beggar?" (99). Most of the townsfolk, therefore, insist that the seeing man is someone else; the stability of their world requires the blind beggar still to be blind, still to beg, still to be the scapegoat for all that is wrong with the world.

Now McTyre moves on to the strife between the man and the

Pharisees.[5] They cannot afford to let the world change, so they do their best to discredit the man. Yet, seeing clearly now in a more than physical way, the man speaks up and speaks back, insisting that his sight could not have been restored unless his healer, Jesus, were "from God."

At this point, McTyre steps back from the story momentarily to foreground the disturbing claim of the text:

That's it! The ultimate threat! It is God who is behind all this spitting in the dirt. It is God who wants liberation, new life, re-creation for human beings. It is God who disrupts the Sabbath and disrupts the world—who keeps things from getting back to normal. (101)

Defending themselves against this unthinkably disturbing possibility, the religious authorities "revert to the safety of the old world and bring back the [original] assumption of the disciples as if the world had not changed. [They tell him,] '*You [blind man] were born entirely in sins*' . . . and drive him out" (101).

Wisely, McTyre turns toward her conclusion, *not* by explaining the new possibility that this story lays before us, but by *showing* it, through Jesus's final encounter with the healed man. The man, who in a sense now truly meets Jesus for the first time, responds, "Lord, I believe!" and worships (v. 38). McTyre brings the sermon to its close with a few brief sentences:

There is the old way, and there is the new way. There is darkness, and there is light. There is blindness, and there is sight. Do we risk it all for the one who spits in the dirt, or save the life we have? (102)

With strong storytelling skill McTyre accomplishes three things in this gospel-story-based sermon. First, by following and develop-

---

5. In this sermon, as in many sermons that deal with a story in which the Pharisees are presented as irremediably blind and resistant to Jesus, the danger exists of preaching an anti-Semitic message. If this sermon tilts in that direction, its saving grace is that it is *we* who are as likely as they to resist the new world—not we who "get it" and they who don't.

ing the storyline closely, she draws her listeners inside the dynamics of this story and its world instead of extrapolating from it a handful of doctrinal and moral points. Second, she keeps her listeners *inside* the world of the story at key points, placing us shoulder-to-shoulder with the neighbors, ready to race to the party that doesn't happen, shoulder-to-shoulder with the Pharisees, and, ultimately, shoulder-to-shoulder with the man himself. Third, McTyre steps away from the story at key points to underscore the dynamic of choice into which it draws us.

By employing these strategies, McTyre sets up a productive resonance between the world of the story and her listeners' own worlds, in which they, too, will face the choice to "risk it all" for the world of newness that God has inaugurated in Jesus Christ or to preserve the neat stability of a world in which one can always be safely inside the rules. She allows this story to become imaginative "rehearsal space" for her listeners, testing parallel situations in their own experience that present a choice between two worlds—one of divinely wrought freedom and new life for those bound by circumstances, or one that remains safely tethered to familiar prejudices. By engaging the story frame by frame, McTyre makes it more likely that this story will become part of that deep wisdom on which her listeners may draw in the future as they venture their own improvisational witness before a world that may prefer to stay blind to the newness of God's work around them.

| CLAUDETTE ANDERSON COPELAND, "TAMAR'S TORN ROBE"[6]

Copeland begins her sermon, based on the story in 2 Samuel 13 of the rape of Tamar by her brother Amnon, not with the biblical story, but with the immediate experience of her listeners—specifically, the unresolved issues and damaging events that can lie hidden in our own histories—our family histories and our personal histories.

6. Claudette Anderson Copeland, "Tamar's Torn Robe," in *This Is My Story: Testimonies and Sermons of Black Women in Ministry*, ed. Cleophus J. LaRue (Louisville: Westminster John Knox, 2005), 113–18. In the paragraphs that follow, page references from this sermon are given in parentheses in the text.

Setting up expectation for where her sermon will lead us, Copeland observes that one of the main reasons we need the "family of God" is to provide us with "an opportunity to redeem, repair, refashion, and yes, reuse" what our family histories have left to us. Copeland paints a picture of the tireless and essential effort that generations of women have poured into building and sustaining their churches. And yet women of the church, observes Copeland, may secretly carry "a past that we did not bargain for, and one we need the Lord to undo." Sometimes, the secrets buried in one's family history can "pollute a woman's present" (113). Copeland issues a challenge: family secrets need to be faced, stories told, wounds uncovered. "I invite you, today, to participate in your own redemption" (114).

With this backdrop in place, Copeland turns to the biblical text at hand. Copeland uses a technique of narrative interpolation—that is, splicing into the biblical story, as it is told, details of contemporary experience—to establish the relevance of Tamar's experience to that of her listeners. For example, in Tamar's story and in the world of her listeners, there are honorable men and there are men who are not trustworthy. There is Jonadab, who enables Amnon to act abusively toward his sister; and there are law-enforcement officers and judges (an interpolation of contemporary reality into the story) who do not think male violence against women needs to be taken seriously. There is Amnon, with his sense of entitlement, and there is the "professor," the male partner, and even the "preacher man" who believes that "women exist as property and as playmates" (115).

Copeland reviews the story only briefly, trusting that it is vivid enough, read once, to be memorable. Listeners with a less firm grasp on the stories of the Old Testament than Copeland's African American congregation may need more help to locate the story, chronologically and in terms of its likely historical setting, in the canon. At the same time, preachers need to recognize (as Copeland no doubt did) that this story is disturbing enough to trigger flashbacks for victims of sexual violence; it should not be overtold with dramatic embellishment of the threat, the struggle, the rape. Listeners need to be given the chance to find their own nearness to, or distance from, the violence of the encounter between Tamar and Amnon.

Tamar flees from the room, her torn robe in her hands, crying out in the agony of the violation of the body, the tearing of the spirit, and the destruction of trust. Ultimately, Tamar's torn robe becomes the story of Tamar condensed into a single image, testifying both to the story's tragedy and the potential carried within it for a reclamation of selfhood. Tamar uses her torn robe as material evidence of the violence perpetrated against her. The robe itself bears witness, and it represents Tamar's refusal to be silenced in the aftermath of her rape. Tamar refuses to hide her torn robe or to silence her voice. She flees to the home of her brother Absalom where (in contrast to the robe itself) she hides for a while. But at last she refuses to suppress the truth.

Copeland allows the robe to become the link between Tamar's story and the stories of her listeners, a symbol of both tragedy and redemption that needs to be "carried" into each listener's present reality:

> Tamar comes out! Damage has been done, we have been sinned against, some things have been torn. . . . But as Tamar, we can come out. She comes out of [Amnon's] house *with her robe*. Torn, but hers. The testimony of her survival. (118)

Tamar becomes empowered when, like the robe itself, she refuses to be hidden away and, despite the risk of retaliation, bears witness to a concrete event of violent tearing that has had profound personal and social consequences. As she cries out, her healing already begins. Evidence in hand, she refuses to be silenced and demands justice.

Copeland hands the torn robe to her listeners. It symbolizes the damaged "created purpose" and personal integrity of all women who have been the victims of violation. The torn robe testifies to all the "tearing"—the violations and violence, emotional and physical—that victims both within and beyond Copeland's congregation have suffered (116).

At the close of the sermon, Copeland challenges her listeners to begin the process of restoration by bearing witness to the long-secreted stories of violation and violence that they, like Tamar, may have tried to hide: "Grab your torn-up robe. You are about to trade it in! . . . Try the knob of [Amnon's] door . . ." (116). The active verbs are essential here: "grab," "trade in," "try the knob." Having urged her listeners to make Tamar's story their own, Copeland urges them to act.

Copeland's sermon is a persuasive demonstration of the way that handing listeners the visual and dynamic elements of a story, rather than a set of concepts, can empower them to grapple with their own lived experience. Copeland's aim is not simply to impart information, but to ignite imaginative rehearsal of the self-reclamation and divine redemption that could be if long-buried secrets are faced and exposed. To reach that goal, Copeland invites her listeners to close the gap between Tamar's story and their own, seeing their own lives as places where they have struggled with dishonorable people, had innocence violated and trust broken, and experienced tragic, body- and soul-damaging events. And yet, just as Tamar's story does not end there, neither must theirs. Listeners, as well as victims they know and love, can "grab the torn robe" of violation hidden in the closets of memory and "lift [their] voice."

With the device of the torn robe and the stories, biblical and personal, that it evokes, Copeland has made the empowering message of her sermon portable enough to make it into the street with her listeners, portable enough to carry into their homes and their everyday relationships, and there to name evil for what it is, reclaim dignity, and call out for truth-telling and justice.

Sermon Strategy II: Align a Biblical Narrative with a Single, Contemporary Situation

| Dr. Jacqueline Lapsley, "Sweating in the Winepress"[7]

Professor of Old Testament Jacqueline Lapsley preached her sermon in early October to a relatively full chapel of seminary students—

7. Jacqueline Lapsley, "Sweating in the Winepress" (sermon preached in Miller Chapel, Princeton Theological Seminary, October 7, 2007); audio recording, Media Library, Princeton Theological Seminary.

juniors, middlers, and seniors—as well as administrators and faculty members. Her text, read by a student shortly before Professor Lapsley stood to preach, was the story in Judges 6 of Gideon's being encountered by a heavenly visitor while he is threshing wheat in a winepress, hiding the crop from Midianite raiders who, we've learned, are routinely stealing the ripe grain out of the field.

But Lapsley doesn't start with the biblical story; she tells the students in the pews a little of their own story. She begins by inviting them—in a tone with a signature touch of wry humor in it!—to remember how this year began, with those "back to school rituals of September . . . the *newness* of everything!—new teachers, new classes, new courses, new *notebooks*! [her tone is all but rhapsodic, and a chuckle ripples through the sanctuary]." The tone tongue-in-cheek, Lapsley continues,

> All these things offer a new start: a chance to begin again. To not repeat the errors of the past. To forge a *new* beginning—perhaps even a new part of ourselves that we half believe lies within us—but has not appeared to date. A person who is better organized; a better student; a better friend, a better Christian.

Lapsley pauses for a beat or two, indicating the passage of time in this state of high and holy aspiration, before she goes on:

> Then about the second or third week of the semester—in fact, right about *now* [more laughter], we feel this window of opportunity beginning to close. The shine begins to wear off of everything—the notebooks have smudges on them, and the clay feet of our fellow-students, even of our teachers, begin to appear.
>
> Deadlines loom—papers and assignments coming at you at high velocity!!—and suddenly, *you find yourself in a deranged version of that arcade game Whack-a-Mole!!* [roar from the students] Each assignment is a mole, but every time you whack one, another pops up!!—until you're whacking, whacking!! [she demonstrates]—but you and your academic mallet: you just can't keep up.
>
> You've worked up a sweat, and you're wondering how all the promise of September has finally come to this.

At this point in the sermon, Lapsley has named, accurately (and with humor), the frustration and doubt that all too soon can set in for seminarians, especially first-year students who sailed in on high tides of hopefulness and a sense of call, only to find themselves behind, frustrated, and filled with doubt a few short weeks into their seminary experience.

Lapsley's transition to the story of Gideon is masterfully simple and smooth: "Gideon, too, is sweating . . . in the winepress."

Lapsley describes the conditions that have forced Gideon to thresh wheat in the winepress, and the low morale of the nation at this point in its history. Echoing her recent phrase about the "promise of September," Lapsley refers to the "promise of the land," and how "they are *in* it now, but it's not how it's supposed to be." She describes, in brief, concrete language, the disappointments of the promised land and the Midianite raids. A skilled preacher, Lapsley does not say "they were disappointed"; she describes the conditions that discourage. *We*—her listeners—will automatically supply the emotional reaction.

Keeping the tone straightforward and colloquial (almost, but not quite, as if we were hearing Gideon's thoughts), Lapsley notes,

> You're not supposed to beat wheat in a winepress; that is not what winepresses are *for*. But you can't beat it out in the open; the Midianites will get it!
>
> Life in the promised land is nothing like they expected.

Lapsley's segue to the dialogue with the angelic visitor is, again, seamless:

> So Gideon is frightened and sweaty and hiding when suddenly a divine visitor appears, whom Gideon does not recognize as divine.
>
> "The Lord is with you, mighty warrior!"

What we can sense, but not see, is Lapsley's imitation of Gideon's astonishment at this form of address—craning his neck, searching the room for this so-called mighty warrior.

Gideon's reply is a tirade of disappointed rage:

"Who, *me*? You're talking to *me*?? I don't see any mighty warriors! And if 'the Lord is with us,' why has all this happened to us? Where are all God's wonderful deeds of the past?? Where is the Lord *now*?!"

Lapsley reminds us of the things—despite his "withering bitterness"—Gideon already knows. Recently, a prophet had visited Israel, she reminds us. He had reviewed before the people the story they all know, the story they have *always* known—the story of the kindness and deliverance of the Lord. But the prophet also reminded them of the condition of continued blessing, that the nation not turn aside to other gods. But, of course, Israel *has* turned aside, and they are reaping the consequences; and amid these conditions, "Gideon's trust in the story has faltered." Knowing this—knowing what Gideon knows—the heavenly messenger continues, undeterred: "Go in this might of yours, and deliver Israel."

Now Lapsley vocalizes what may be the skeptical query of her listeners: "This 'might' of yours?? What might is that? Gideon's anger? His tenacity?? (He keeps on beating that wheat!)"

Gideon, says Lapsley, "offers the customary demurrals" in response to this call of God; but his excuses don't prevail. Instead, Gideon gets a promise: "I, the Lord, will be with you. I'll be with you. . . . Is not my very act of sending you a sign of my commitment?" Expanding the text slightly and contemporizing, Lapsley is not just telling Gideon's story, but ours, too. Turning to the here and now of seminary life, Lapsley brings her sermon to a deft conclusion:

> Gideon goes on to have a mixed career; he doesn't get everything right, not by a long shot. But he understands that God's commitment to Israel still holds. He recognizes that God's faithfulness in the past is enough to go forward on.
>
> And for us, sweating in our own winepresses, this is good news indeed.

Lapsley's sermon—only nine and a half minutes long—is a model of spare storytelling that does not dwell on unnecessary detail but supplies just enough action and dialogue to keep us riveted to this encounter. She builds this sermon on an underlying, classic structure of narrative (which happens, in this case to be the structure of the biblical scene itself). The sermon begins with trouble in our (seminary) world, presents similar trouble in Gideon's world, and then allows the trouble to intensify.

Notably, the appearance of the angelic visitor *does not "fix" Gideon's situation*; the angelic message is *more* trouble, not its resolution—a key factor in the expert handling of this sermon. The angelic summons for Gideon to vanquish the Midianites sounds like a taunt, under the circumstances; it only enrages and embitters Gideon.

Next, there is a short retrospective about the story of promise that has been the story of Israel, and it is at this point that Lapsley picks up for us the promissory clue that will change this downward spiral: "I will be with you! Is not the very fact that I am calling you a sign of my commitment?"

Then, in a few light strokes of the brush, Lapsley turns first Gideon's story, and then ours, too, toward hope: "The story of God's faithfulness in the past is enough to go on . . . good news indeed."

Best Practices for Handling Narrative Material in Sermons

Handling narratives well in preaching is something of an art. It takes practice, but it is a skill that can be learned. Staying attentive to four guidelines will go a long way toward helping narratives function for listeners as lively, multidimensional imaginative rehearsal for everyday action.

First, good narrative preachers set their listeners down (so to speak) *inside* the story's world, instead of observing or analyzing the story from *outside*. Second, good narrative preachers help their listeners *discover and explore* the dynamics of a story; they do not *explain* the story. Third, good narrative preachers often report action in short, simple subject/verb sentences, and in what we call *narrative present tense*. Fourth, good narrative preachers report dialogue with minimal intrusion on the dialogical material itself. We'll elaborate on these one by one.

1. Good narrative preachers set their listeners down *inside* the world of the story, instead of observing or analyzing the story from *outside*.

Telling stories well is such an important skill that I typically begin a course in basic preaching by assigning students specific narrative texts that they then work on together. They engage the text from many different angles through exercises like group *lectio divina* (a process of reflective, meditative reading), *blocking* the text as a dramatic scene together, or *talking back* to the text from the point of view of listeners representing very different social locations and experience frames (unemployed single parent on food stamps, aging widower, young adult skeptical of religion in general, person dealing with physical disability, junior-high-age kid, female corporate executive, etc.). We discuss in class good ways to get sermons underway, and we listen to examples. Yet, inevitably, there will be the student who starts her sermon on, say, Mark's story of the forgiveness/healing of the paralytic let down through the roof, "When we consider this pericope from Mark's Gospel . . ."! As an invitation to get inside the story at hand and start looking around, this is a nonstarter. This opening phrase signals we're in for a dry, detached analysis of the text, and you can feel the listeners wrestling to overcome the temptation to simply check out. Another beginning is slightly stronger: "Imagine what it would have been like to be in the crowd that day . . ." Certainly, this invitation to imagine being "on scene" is stronger than the previous opener, but it still assumes that we are standing outside the story, outside the world of the story, and must exercise an act of fantasy to insert ourselves into the setting and scene of action.

Far better is a beginning that simply assumes that we are *already* in the setting and situation: "Jesus is in town. Four friends lug a paralyzed comrade through the streets on his pallet, but when they get to the house, the crowd packed around the open door is six deep. 'Look, this guy needs help!' yells the sweaty friend gripping the mat's front corner. But nobody even gives him a glance; in fact, the crowd packs itself tighter into the doorway. Another of the four carriers mutters a curse—then: 'The roof, *now*. We're going up . . .'"

This beginning places us, the listeners, in the middle of the scene. We see key details, smell the sweat, and hear the urgent dialogue of the paralytic's anxious friends. The details are enough to let us find our bearings and become invested in what will happen next.

An alternative would be to delay beginning the biblical narrative and instead introduce a contemporary story: "Like thousands of other mothers fleeing their war-torn villages, a young African woman trudges into the clearing where United Nations relief workers have set up a feeding station, her pitifully weak toddler whimpering on her back. She can *see* the food, but she cannot get near it. She sees not just dozens but hundreds of others who have gotten here first, etc." Notice that, here again, we are set down by the storyteller in the *middle* of the story, and the narrative present tense is used, although clearly this is a story that was perhaps reported on the news sometime in the recent past. This beginning evokes the sense of desperation on behalf of another's need that sets up the story in Mark 2. One might segue to the text with a single phrase, "Driven by exactly such desperation, four men are tearing apart the roof of a house. Somewhere below them is the teacher who is their only hope."

2. Good narrative preachers help listeners *discover and explore* a story's possibilities. They do not prescribe how listeners "ought" to feel, or flatten the story into a set of propositions.

Narratives are a distinctive form of discourse. They convey meaning in a way different from discourses comprised of concepts or precepts. Stories cannot be distilled into a list of ideas or insights without loss, since they convey meaning through the dynamic interaction of their structural elements. Every story is a dynamic interaction of (1) a setting and situation; (2) distinctive characters and their capacity to act [agency]; and (3) plot and telos [that toward which the plot aims]. If a story is well told, and if the perspective of the listener on that story is managed well, there will be no need to spell out the insights gained in experiencing the story or to wring a moral out of it. This is true, in part, because we master the skills of listening to stories and sensing the interaction of their elements at an early age.

To preach well on biblical narratives, a preacher needs to (a) *trust* the capacity of the listener to make sense of a story; (b) trust the narrative to evoke insight; and (c) resist the temptation to step outside the narrative frame to make points and thereby control what the listener makes of the story. This doesn't mean that the preacher has no aims in his or her presentation of the narrative; rather, it means that he or she will adopt a particular perspective from which to view the action and stick with it long enough to allow it to yield insights that are best gained from that particular angle of vision before switching to another angle of vision. On the whole, one can at most manage two different angles of vision within a narrative before listeners become victims of a sort of narrative "whiplash."

Yes—stories may be used by preachers to illustrate points; but that is not what we mean by helping listeners become familiar with the narrative backbone of the canon. Biblical narratives become resources for creative imagination and action when our listeners experience them as multidimensional "worlds" of experience.

A preacher skillful at leading her listeners into the world of a narrative (and all biblical narratives evoke a "world" of assumptions and possibilities, even if they are as brief as a one-verse parable) is not in the business of making doctrinal points, but of developing in listeners the capacity to become coexplorers of the text who can draw their own valid insights from their experience with a story. Part of the richness of the parables of Jesus is that their meaning is open ended.

Furthermore, the world of experience that a parable assumes and evokes interacts with the reader's or listener's *own* experience. It is in this dynamic resonance between "worlds" of narrated meaning—between storylines in Scripture and the ongoing "story" of experience—that imaginative possibilities for faithful patterns of action emerge.

3.   Good storytellers speak in short, direct sentences (subject + verb + direct object), often using what is known as *narrative present tense.*

Skillful storytellers report action in short, brisk, direct sentences. They avoid long introductory clauses (phrases beginning with words like *although, in light of the fact,* and so forth). They avoid sentences that include lists—a series of nouns, verbs, or verbal phrases separated by commas. And they often speak in narrative present tense, even if they're reporting something that happened yesterday.

Say, for example, you're having coffee with friends and want to tell them about something funny your little niece said over lunch last weekend. You *could* say, "Although my niece, the daughter of my oldest brother, has not even yet turned three, she turned to me at lunch last weekend and declared, 'This cheese is delectable!' This was so amusing I nearly choked on the chicken soup I was eating at the time." It hardly needs to be said that this is very clumsy storytelling. It's more likely that you would say something like this: "So, last weekend I'm out for lunch with my brother and his kids, and the littlest one—a little redhead who's not even three yet!—looks up at me and says, 'This cheese is *delectable!*'" (No comment on your difficulty swallowing your soup is necessary; everybody gets the surprise factor.) Notice that you use present tense to describe a past incident; this gives your account a feeling of immediacy. You note her red hair (which contributes a visual distinctiveness to the scene) and her age (necessary to the impact of what she says) by way of an interjection—an interrupting phrase. Most important, you don't report your reaction; you let the accent on the word *delectable* underscore the surprise factor. You trust your listeners to "get" it.

Too often, preachers tell stories from the pulpit with deadening detail. Instead of trusting that a well-told incident evokes its own reaction, they feel compelled to explain how *they* reacted, or worse, say something like "Isn't that surprising?"—as if their listeners were too dim-witted to make sense of a story they hear.

In general, storytelling from the pulpit is more successful if it is colloquial and conversational. When a vignette is well sketched, there is no need to explain what it "means" or to dictate to listeners what to make of the story.

4.   Good preachers report dialogue with minimal dialogue-markers (phrases like, "he remarked," "she replied," etc.).

Read aloud to yourself these two versions of the same incident, which includes a brief conversational exchange between a mother and child:

Take 1

A little boy of seven had gotten up late. He was late for the bus.

His mother said to him with impatience, "Hurry now, here is the bus. You may miss it if you don't hurry. Where is your lunchbox?"

The little boy dropped his eyes and mumbled, "I lost it."

Astonished, his mother replied, "You *lost* it? But that is now the third lunchbox you have lost, and it is only October. We bought you a special Yogi Bear lunchbox, and now you have lost it. Your sister had only one lunch bucket all the way through elementary school. Why can't you be more like your sister?"

The little boy looked ashamed. His shoulders slumped, and it looked as if he might cry.

Angry, his mother said sharply, "Well, I don't care if you even have a lunch! There is the bus. Now, go on!"

And she pushed him out the door toward the street.

Take 2

"C'mon—you're late for the bus! Here's your lunch—where's your lunchbox? What'd you do with it??"

[no pause] "What d'you mean you 'lost' it?? That's the third one you've lost!—and it's only *October!!* We buy you a special Yogi Bear lunchbox and what do *you* do? You go and lose it! Why can't you be more like your sister?? Go on, now—there's the bus! I don't care if you even *have* a lunch."

While take 1 accurately reports the action, the second version of the scene captures our attention and is far more involving. It is involving because we feel ourselves being addressed; *we* are in the role of the child, the target of this barrage from his frustrated, angry parent. We don't hear a word from the child, and the preacher has provided no visual picture. He doesn't need to; the language and tone alone allow us to "see" the increasing hurt, the slumped shoulders, the crumpling expression on the child's face.

The second version, taken from a recording of a sermon by Fred Craddock, also lacks any dialogue markers ("he said," "she said"). In the recording, Craddock conveys the tone of the scene with nuances of his voice. This is a skill that takes time to develop, but it keeps us inside the story instead of allowing us to remain safely distanced from the tension of the situation. Listeners feel the impact of what is going on personally and are deeply invested in what is to come. We yearn for some move toward resolution in this damaged relationship—and Craddock delivers a scene of healing reconciliation a few lines later.[8]

Narrative Preaching Strategies and Improvisational Imagination

Every day, Christians' imaginations are influenced, like everyone else's, by dozens of storylines—read on the web, seen on television, or witnessed unfolding around them. Many listeners come to worship hoping—even expecting—to hear stories. Some may hope to be entertained; but nearly all will hope to hear stories in which they can recognize themselves—their feelings and motivations, their dilemmas and failures, their fears and their hopes.

Above all, people come to worship to hear stories, biblical and otherwise, that project on the screen of their imaginations a *particular kind* of world: a world reframed by divine redemptive action and divine promise. They come for a chance to imaginatively rehearse what it might look like to act inventively and faithfully in the ordinary situations they encounter every day, participating in God's ongoing drama of redemptive transformation. Our sermons can offer them that chance.

8. Fred B. Craddock, "If at the Altar You Remember" (chapel sermon preached at Princeton Theological Seminary); audio recording, Media Library, Princeton Theological Seminary.

Further Reading: The Role of Story and Narration in Christian Theology and Preaching

The literature generated by the "turn toward narrative" in the late twentieth and early twenty-first centuries is vast. These works acquaint the reader with some seminal essays and works in theology and preaching. Again, these works are informed by a range of varied biblical-hermeneutical, theological, and homiletical commitments.

Graves, Michael. *The Story of Narrative Preaching: Experience and Exposition: A Narrative*. Eugene, OR: Cascade, 2015.

Hauerwas, Stanley, and L. Gregory Jones, eds. *Why Narrative? Readings in Narrative Theology*. Grand Rapids: Eerdmans, 1989.

Lowry, Eugene L. *The Homiletical Plot*. Rev. ed. Louisville: Westminster John Knox, 2001.

———. *The Sermon: Dancing the Edge of Mystery*. Nashville: Abingdon, 1997.

Robinson, Wayne Hadley, ed. *Journey toward Narrative Preaching*. New York: Pilgrim, 1990.

Thiemann, Ronald F. *Revelation and Theology: The Gospel as Narrated Promise*. Notre Dame: University of Notre Dame Press, 1990.

Wright, John W. *Telling God's Story: Narrative Preaching for Christian Formation*. Downers Grove, IL: InterVarsity Academic, 2007.

CHAPTER 6

Sermons That Travel: How Metaphor Reveals Sight Lines of Redemptive Hope

In the previous three chapters, we considered how strategic use of some familiar elements of sermon composition can help those in our pews become bolder agents of redemptive interruption in the situations and spaces they deal with every day.

First, choosing to interpret both the world and biblical texts through a hermeneutical lens of divine promise (chapter 3) grants preacher and listener alike "bifocal" or "stereoscopic" vision. Such vision allows us to see ordinary situations for what they *are*—places of brokenness, missed opportunities, deeply embedded prejudices, self-absorbed greed, and systematic oppression. Yet stereoscopic vision allows us to see these very same situations as arenas where God is present and active, summoning our participation in the redemptive process.

Second, sermons that invite the listener into more theologically mindful, self-aware participation in distinctive Christian practices (chapter 4) assist our listeners in developing a repertoire of theologically laden patterns of action on which to draw amid the challenging situations they encounter in their weekday lives. Self-aware participation in their congregations' practices of worship, fellowship, care, decision-making, and witness inscribes into Christians' bodily, material experience paradigms for witness that is rooted deep in Christian tradition, yet responds creatively to the demands of the moment. Third, when stories in our sermons do more than illustrate doctrinal or moral concepts, when they function as spaces of imaginative rehearsal for participating in the ongoing, redemptive work of God (chapter 5), we assist listeners in the kind of experimental, anticipatory imagination that is prerequisite to all creative action, including actions that bear witness to the inclusive love, restorative justice, and healing mercy of God.

The present chapter ventures into what may be less familiar territory for some preachers. Here, we focus on sermons constructed around a particular rhetorical trope: metaphor.[1] Devoting so much attention to a single figure of speech may strike some readers as odd. Historically, theologians (and, in their wake, preachers) have often harbored a mistrust of metaphor as a mode of speech that is untrustworthy and evasive; but these prejudices are unwarranted. Far from concealing or blurring true insight, metaphors have the capacity to reveal insights that cannot be reduced to a series of propositions. There is considerable evidence for this in Scripture itself.

Biblical writers turn again and again to metaphor to express the dynamics of God's redemptive work in the world, both the dynamics of judgment and the dynamics of deliverance. Prophetic writings are saturated with powerful similes (phrases using *like* or *as*) and metaphors, which simply connect two unlike fields of meaning (for example, "God is a consuming fire"), a semantic (meaning-producing) effect we'll explore in more detail below.

A second reason to pay attention to and master the use of metaphor in the pulpit is that even the most cursory scan of the sermons of effective, prophetic preachers makes abundantly clear that using powerful metaphors is an often-shared trait among preachers whose aim is to mobilize Christian witness in challenging situations. Third—and this may be the most compelling reason

1. In homiletical literature, the most thorough treatment of metaphor in preaching is Rodney Kennedy's book *The Creative Power of Metaphor: A Rhetorical Homiletics* (Lanham, MD: University Press of America, 1993), which proposes metaphor as the basis for what Kennedy terms a "rhetorical" homiletics. Kennedy sketches a basic overview of developments in metaphor theory and ultimately privileges (as do I) Paul Ricoeur's elucidation of the unique semantics of metaphor. However, Kennedy's understatement of the crucial, dialectical play of the simultaneous assertions, *is* and *is not,* at the heart of a metaphor leaves his presentation of the distinctive semantics of metaphor somewhat unclear. Also, Kennedy understates the theological and methodological implications of his rhetorical homiletic.

of all, given our concerns in these pages—the semantic dynamics of metaphorical expression are such that metaphors *are not only memorable for listeners; they are also portable.* In other words—to speak metaphorically!—when we preach a sermon wrapped around a well-chosen metaphor, we hand listeners a powerful navigational instrument that can reveal sight lines of hope amid complex, everyday situations. A well-crafted metaphor functions as a key to unlock imagination, aligning biblical witness and contemporary context, historical example and present-day opportunity, in a way that generates fresh ways of seeing a situation and new pathways of creative, improvisational agency within it.

Metaphor: Not to Be Trusted?

Some preachers are inclined to be suspicious of metaphor. A couple of years ago, I was invited to teach on homiletics at a theological conference for pastors, and I chose to teach on why and how we can build sermons around metaphor. I decided to test the waters, so to speak (another metaphor!), by writing "using metaphor in sermons" on the whiteboard and asking the pastors what came first to mind in response to the phrase.

A veteran preacher in a stiff collar had a strong opinion: "I'd never use metaphor in a sermon if I could help it. A metaphor is just a muddy, unclear way of saying something when you were too lazy to do the hard work of being clear!" He settled with a huff into his chair.

A young preacher wearing what looked like a brand-new suit raised her hand. "Isn't talking in metaphors sort of sneaky?" she asked. "My folks just want me to tell them what to do."

The blue-jean-clad pastoral-team leader from the GenX fellowship next to the college campus in town was sitting behind her, nodding vigorously. "Why say something 'pretty' and contrived when some smart high-tech visuals can make crystal-clear theological concepts just *pop* off the screen?"

I was fascinated (and, to be honest, a little taken aback) by the vehemence of these opinions; but more than that, I was curious about the assumptions and prejudices lying behind them. I'm happy to say that some more sympathetic push-back soon followed, with preachers around the room telling about sermons built on metaphors, ones they'd heard or developed themselves, and how those sermons stayed in their memories when so many others had long since been forgotten.

I began teasing out of the group some of the assumptions that lay behind the resistance in the room to using metaphor in the pulpit. These included the belief that a metaphor is deliberate rhetorical evasion of truth, that metaphor conceals truth, that a metaphor is merely a "show-off" way of saying something (and therefore amounts to homiletical grandstanding), and that there is nothing one could say through metaphor that cannot be said equally well in a few straightforward propositions.

Yet I was unconvinced, as were others in the room. What if, some asked, a metaphor can actually reveal truths that *cannot be shown otherwise*? What if a well-turned metaphor *can reveal previously unseen possibilities in familiar situations* in a manner unique to this figure of speech? What if the fact of the matter is that a metaphor can connect the dynamics of a present situation with future possibilities *far more efficiently* than heaped-up prose or a list of examples? These are my hunches, based on my own experience with hearing, remembering, and acting on metaphor-driven sermons, as well as beginning to craft them and observe their lasting impact. In a moment, we'll consider Paul Ricoeur's work on metaphor, which supports possibilities for metaphor these queries suggest; but first, a simple example from the point of view of sermon listeners may clarify how metaphors work.

Two church members, Eric and Janice, run into one another in the produce section of the local supermarket. Their sons are on the same soccer team, so they exchange greetings and talk briefly about the kids. Then Janice changes the subject: "So, Eric, I missed church last Sunday; we were out of town. What was the sermon about?"

We can imagine several possible responses on Eric's part, depending on what happened during last Sunday's sermon. A not-too-surprising response might be, "Gee, you know, I can't remember. It was interesting at the time, but—darn. I just don't know." Another might be, "I took notes on my phone; do you want me to send them?" This implies that the sermon conveyed information worth capturing and sharing; and that's a good thing.

But here's another possible response: "You know, I don't remember all the details, but the Scripture had something to do with what it was like for the people of God to be in exile. The preacher described different situations today that are 'exile' experiences. Experiences like losing your job, having a marriage end, suddenly finding you're really sick. Then she picked up on all that recent news about refugees huddled on the border, how they can't go home, but there's no home waiting for them here, either. That must be terrible—and scary.

"I remember the exile thing, I guess, because I kept thinking about it: how my mother felt exiled from all their old social circles when my dad's dementia got bad, and how my brother-in-law felt like an exile around the church when his marriage broke up. I guess exile is whenever you feel you've lost whatever counted as home. And the preacher talked about how God didn't abandon the people during the exile; they knew they counted with God, and that gave them hope. Made me wonder how churches could do better with guys like my brother-in-law."

Janice wasn't there Sunday morning, but Eric's report interests her; she picks up the thread.

"Exile. That's a really good description of what it felt like when I was a kid and my mother took us kids and left the house, because my dad was drinking then and he could get so violent. We lived in shelters for a while. I felt like an outsider everywhere. Everyone treated us like homelessness was a disease. That was exile."

"Wow," says Eric, "I had no idea. That must have been tough."

"It was, but it makes me want to do something for the refugee families the papers say are coming to *our* area. I know what it's like to feel like you've been thrown into a strange universe, and you're disoriented and homesick. And nobody cares; they won't even make eye contact."

Notice how the conversation opens up when the sermon has been built on a metaphor. It is not the details of the sermon that Eric remembers. But the sermon's central metaphor, "exile," *did* stay with him. Now, several days later, he is not only able to continue to explore different experiences with this imaginative key; but he also doesn't have to say much before Janice, too, is able to think productively using the metaphorical lens Eric has handed on to her.

Before turning to the homiletical practicalities of choosing and using metaphors in preaching, we need first to consider what gives metaphors their unique capacity to generate fresh insights in relation to new situations.

What Is a Metaphor and How Does It Work?

Metaphors are not particularly exotic, nor are they the exclusive domain of poets. As a matter of fact, we naturally use metaphors of place, time, and action in everyday, conversational speech. When someone asks you how you liked your winter getaway to a tropical island, and you enthuse, "It was paradise!" you are not speaking literally; you are using a (fairly common) metaphor of place. When the newscaster announces that politicians are "locked" in "eleventh-hour" negotiations, she is speaking metaphorically; she is not saying that someone has locked all the legislators in a room, and it is 11:00 p.m. Of course, these are very common metaphorical expressions— so common, in fact, that they have ceased to be very arresting or thought provoking. We call such well-worn metaphorical expressions *dead* metaphors; and they are actually better avoided in the pulpit, since they do not coax our imaginations into active mode.

As a trope, or figure of speech, metaphor is often confused with some of its near grammatical cousins. These closely related tropes include image-crafting, simile, analogy, and allegory.

Much has been made of the importance of using visual imagery in preaching, and rightly so. Images allow the sermon to communicate not only audially (through hearing), but also visually. An image can show what can't be entirely captured in conceptual language. It can juxtapose visual elements in ways that enlighten or disturb us. Consider, for example, an image—one of many such images you've no doubt seen on the news. In the foreground, her face turned away from us, is a skinny teenager balancing a toddler on her hip.

Her clothes are ragged. Her feet are planted in what appears to be a trash dump, and she has in her hand—implausibly—a half-inflated children's pool toy in the shape of a unicorn. We can also see in the near distance what appear to be makeshift tents. In the far distance, gleaming in the setting sun, several multimillion-dollar mansions dot the green hillside. Next to most of them, large luminous blue patches indicate exotically shaped swimming pools. Without words, the image focuses our thoughts on vast economic disparities, the contrast between lives of daily struggle and daily leisure, and a deep sense of irony.

While images do important work in sermons—illustrating concepts, evoking feeling, conveying irony—using images does not, in itself, make the sermon metaphorical. Eloquently describing a tree does not make the tree a metaphor. We can describe a breathtaking sunset and then say that it inspires in us an awe akin to what we feel when contemplating the power of God; but, as moving as the scene may be, the inspiring effect of this visual strategy should not be confused with metaphor.

Two other near cousins of metaphor are *simile* and *analogy*. A simile is any comparison that makes use of the word *like* or similar words of direct comparison. "God's forgiveness is like showers falling on dry earth" is a simile—a comparison. Closely related is analogy, which is, in a sense, an extended simile. An example of simple analogy would be, "As a bird shelters her young in the cold, so God shelters us in our aloneness." Some analogies can be quite extended. A biblical analogy that occurs again and again compares Israel's relationship to the Lord God to the relationship between vineyard and vinedresser.

Another related trope is *allegory*. Allegory is an analogy pressed further, so that every feature of one type of experience is made to correspond, explicitly, with a single feature of another realm of experience. In Mark 4:10–20, Jesus is portrayed working out the parable of the sower as an allegory of the spreading of the gospel and its fruits. John Bunyan's classic religious novel, *Pilgrim's Progress*, is another example of allegory.

So far, we've clarified what a metaphor, or a metaphorical expression, is *not*. Specifying what a metaphor actually *is* has proven a more difficult proposition, even among philosophers of language. Here we return to the work of Paul Ricoeur, whose thought we have encountered earlier. Although metaphor has been a subject of scholarly interest since the time of Aristotle, Ricoeur advanced the twentieth-century discussion dramatically, identifying points of weakness or confusion in older theories and then constructing his own proposal. Readers who wish to explore Ricoeur's work on this subject in detail will be well repaid by the effort; for present purposes, a summary of his main ideas will be sufficient.[2]

First, Ricoeur rejects the notion that metaphor is somehow a "corruption" of speech—a means of linguistic obfuscation—and that a metaphor is therefore either nonserious or deliberately misleading. Next, Ricoeur explains and sets aside several theories of metaphor that, for one reason or another, he finds inadequate. He rejects, for example, the notion that a metaphor is simply a matter of word substitution—using an unexpected word instead of the more usual one—and that its meaning derives from the mental work we have to do to think through the substitution. For example, when I propose to a friend that we "take my chariot" instead of his car to the movies, my substitution of the word "chariot" for "car" is ironic (as anyone familiar with my vehicle knows); and while the word substitution may amuse and I may get a wry smile, it is not especially illuminating. This word substitution doesn't constitute a metaphor.

Rather, Ricoeur proposes, a metaphor is the unexpected juxtaposition of two terms—specifically, two terms that represent *realms of meaning that we do not typically associate with one another*—and makes a statement that, on the surface of things, may not seem to make sense. For example, consider the recently popular child-raising metaphor, *helicopter parent*. This metaphor draws together two semantic fields—that is, two unrelated fields of experience, terminology, and experience. On the one hand, we have the semantic field of parenting styles and, on the other, the characteristics of a particular airborne transport machine, the helicopter. It is actually

2. See Paul Ricoeur, *The Rule of Metaphor: Multidisciplinary Studies of the Creation of Meaning in Language,* trans. Robert Czerny (Toronto: University of Toronto Press, 1977).

not just the juxtaposition of the two *words*, but also the overlay between the two semantic *fields* these terms evoke, that makes the metaphor "work." Considering the behavior and uses of helicopters in relation to parenting is fairly illuminating when we want to talk about a particularly anxious, monitoring type of parenting style. We could "ramp up" (note the metaphor!) our case-making with an example: "When the toddler at the slide was pushed aside by the playground bully, its helicopter mother swooped in on the bully, all fangs and claws." Now the semantic field of frightening-carnivorous-animal behavior has been added; we are "mixing" our metaphors!—which is fine in everyday speech, but not recommended in sermons.

In a true metaphor, there is a missing word that actually links the two terms (and two fields of experience) involved: *is*. We are staking a claim of identity—sameness—which is, in fact, nonsense. Implicitly, we have said, "That parent *is* a helicopter," which is not literally true. We have also asserted, "The toddler's mother *is* a pouncing tiger." Again, she may be scary, but she isn't a large, fierce, black-and-orange-striped predatory cat. Notice that upon hearing the literal assertion *is* that lurks inside these metaphors, we quickly enter a mental caveat: *is not!*

For Ricoeur, that is precisely the point with metaphors. They pull two terms together with *is*, while, at the same time, the two terms semantically repel each other—*is not*. Confronted with the phrase *helicopter parent*, the mind begins immediately to grapple with a statement that, on the face of it, is nonsensical. "No," says our inner literalist, "a parent is not a helicopter." Yet our inner poet demurs: "Not so fast!—there is something revealing here, when I move, mentally, between these two realms of experience—the behavior of parents hovering over their children and the behavior of helicopters hovering above a spot on the ground." This dialectic of *is/is not*, says Ricoeur, provokes productive reflection, causing us to gain insight that we could not have achieved through a careful, rational explanation of parenting styles, their characteristics, and their effects. Furthermore, the latter explanation would be extremely tedious, because it leaves us, the listener, passive. Tedious explanations put our imaginations to sleep, instead of awakening and activating them.

Ricoeur describes metaphor as a *semantic impertinence*. A metaphor is balanced on one small point of similarity (parents and helicopters can both hover over a spot), but there are many points of dissimilarity: parents do not literally fly, or hover in the air, and helicopters do not give birth to and care for small human beings. Yet, in the jostling of the dissimilarities, a whole array of insights quickly jumps to life. A metaphorical turn of phrase activates the imagination of the listener, as we saw with the metaphorical use of *exile* coupled with such familiar experiences as job loss, the ending of a marriage, or the onset of severe illness. The metaphor triggered imaginative exploration and new insight not only for Eric (who heard the sermon), but also for Janice (who did not). A metaphor is a proposal; it invites us to see the familiar *as* something else. This dynamic—this *seeing as*—is, for Ricoeur, the crucial dynamic of metaphorical speech. "Suddenly," writes Ricoeur, "we are seeing as. . . . [W]e see old age as the dusk of day, time as a beggar, nature as a temple with living pillars."[3] Metaphors "reframe" familiar situations, enabling us to see those situations otherwise. For example, the exile metaphor has the potential to reveal something about not only one's own suffering, but also that of others, as Eric's example of refugees "exiled" from home demonstrates.

One may wonder what all of this has to do with Christian preaching. Why should Christian preachers consider building a sermon, from time to time, around a central, sustained metaphor? There are, no doubt, many good reasons, but two in particular stand out. First, metaphors are well attested in Scripture; they are deliberately chosen by biblical writers for their evocative, meaning-generating power. One need only page through a few of the psalms to find one metaphor after another. We will have more to say about this momentarily.

Second, metaphors, because of their semantic open-endedness, are not merely *memorable*; they are *portable*. Often—perhaps *too* often—we stuff our sermons with vivid examples, catchy phrases, or

3. Paul Ricoeur, *From Text to Action: Essays in Hermeneutics, II* (Evanston, IL: Northwestern University Press, 1991), 173.

a series of admonitions all beginning with the letter M in the hope that these strategies will give the sermon a shelf-life in listeners' memory longer than the time it takes them to walk to the parking lot. We hope that in some situation a few days from now, one of our illustrations clicks in, or a listener will remember at a critical moment, just before escalating an argument with his spouse, what we said he "should" do when tempted in this way. These memory-assisting devices do work for some listeners, some of the time. But just as often, they do not. In my view, the reason for this is fairly simple: *the preacher, not the listener, has done all the imaginative work of the sermon.*

When the preacher turns loose a well-chosen metaphor in Sunday's sermon and begins to reveal its creative possibilities, she or he activates a "sight line" of possibility whose trajectory can be imaginatively extended *by the listener* well beyond Sunday into the world of Monday. Both Eric and Janice are able to allow *exile* to reframe familiar experiences (Eric's brother-in-law's sense of being rebuffed by his church and Janice's childhood memories of homelessness), gaining new insight. But more than that, both are able to reframe *others'* experience and, by relating that to their own, begin imagining what active care might look like for the "exiles" living in their own community. Metaphors have remarkable potential to travel with our listeners as they navigate the unique demands of the settings and situations of their lives.

Metaphor in Christian Scripture and Theology

Metaphors, along with simile and analogy, abound in Scripture. Such expressions come into play particularly with reference to the being and action of God, or the relationship between God and the people of Israel. Although simile is somewhat more common—God is said to "wrap himself in light as with a garment" (Ps. 104:2), for example—metaphors are frequent, as well. God is said to "ride the wings of the wind" (Pss. 18:10; 104:3) and declares, "I will inscribe [God's people] on the palms of my hands" (Isa. 49:16). Prophets, too, employ metaphor; Joel's chilling poem in which invading locusts are pictured as a ruthless, disciplined, advancing army is an example.

New Testament literature is also richly metaphorical: "Behold the Lamb of God," "We are the body of Christ," "Put on the whole armor of God." "Our God is a consuming fire," declares the writer of Hebrews (Heb. 12:29, quoting Deut. 4:24). When New Testament writers face the difficult task of shedding light on the meaning of the Christian practices of baptism and the Lord's Supper, they choose metaphorical language. For example, in Romans 6:3-5, Paul draws on the familiar experiences of death and burial in the earth with the baptismal rite. "We have been buried with [Christ] by baptism into death" (v. 4), says Paul. The experience that Paul is trying to help his readers understand (in this case, Christian baptism) is thus "re-framed" by the burial of the dead—a more familiar experience. The plunge under the baptismal waters, especially given that in Paul's day baptism was customarily a full-immersion experience, is "re-framed" as burial of that which is dead—a relinquishment of life. In shorthand, Paul has created a metaphor: *Baptism is burial*. The *is* in the middle of this little sentence is a metaphorical claim, not a literal one. Thus, the relationship that is set up between the two is such that it cannot be resolved into a simple assertion of identity (*is*) or difference (*is not*).[4] Resonances are set up between these two realms of experience, yet the disclosive power of the apostle's metaphor lies in the fact that we cannot resolve the tension set up by the metaphorical claim. The resonance of similarity (plunging into a state or substance that interrupts the breath of life) teases at the mind; this discloses something about baptism—that one kind of life (life subject to death's ultimate claim) is ending, and another is begun. Yet, at the same time, the two experiences refuse to be entirely (literally) conflated.

Biblical writers draw on experiences that would be *familiar* to their readers and align them with the *less* familiar, or somewhat obscure, rites and spiritual dynamics of Christian experience, to

---

4. I have argued similarly concerning preaching on the redemptive import of the cross for human experiences of sin and suffering. See Sally A. Brown, *Cross Talk: Preaching Redemption Here and Now* (Louisville: Westminster John Knox, 2008).

reveal what cannot be conveyed in literal terms. What should not be missed here is that, as biblical writers connect two fields of experience (for example, baptism and burial), the *semantic impertinence* of the metaphor's claim—*baptism is burial with Christ*—produces *productive tension*. That is, the metaphor is *generative of fresh insight* long after we first encounter it. Through the semantic impertinence of metaphor, biblical writers create a productive tension between two realms of experience. Metaphors evoke in us new understanding that no amount of pedantic explanation could produce.[5] Although familiarity has caused many biblical metaphors to be less surprising to us today than they may well have been to those who first heard them, their implications are still illuminating to generation upon generation of believers.

Beyond Memorable to Portable: Why Metaphors of Time, Place, or Action Live beyond Sunday

Good metaphors, with their simultaneous assertion of *is* and *is not*, activate our minds into exploring the overlap and interface of two semantic realms. We are able to articulate something we may have sensed before, but for which we had no name.

When we take an imagination-prompting metaphor with us into contexts our preacher did not even imagine, much less describe, we can still uncover fresh insight. Thus, when an author writes an article about the damaging effects of helicopter parenting, she isn't interested in just imparting some interesting tidbits of information; she is hoping also that some of her readers will be parents and that, for them, the metaphor will prove (as we have been suggesting) not only *memorable* but also *portable*. This is a realistic hope on the author's part; she knows that if a metaphor is at all pertinent to our experience, it will stay with us.

Well-chosen, sustained metaphors in preaching effectively gen-

---

5. As Kennedy states in a succinct summary of the primary characteristics of metaphor, "Metaphor is not reducible to a literal meaning or paraphrase" (*Creative Power of Metaphor*, 60).

erate what I am calling *sight lines of hope*. Sermons built around a central metaphor have a powerful capacity to bridge across contexts—biblical, historical, and contemporary—revealing sight lines of hope that connect past, present, and future, and reveal trajectories of redemptive possibility. My own exploration over the last ten years of dozens of published sermons has revealed something I find striking. Nearly every gifted preacher whose work I regularly consult uses metaphor with some regularity—not all the time (no strategy deserves to be used week after week), but judiciously and effectively.

Furthermore, most metaphor-centered sermons are built on one of three particular types of metaphors: *metaphors of action*, *metaphors of place*, or *metaphors of time*. Perhaps not surprisingly, metaphors of action, place, or time are common not only in biblical and secular literature, but also in ordinary speech. We talk about "the day of reckoning," "the crossroads of decision," and "going for broke"; we say that "time creeps," lament a neighborhood that is a "food desert," and speak of "talking the subject to death."

What follows is a short list of metaphors of action, place, and time that I have heard used in sermons. A caution: you will see that these phrases *do not look like* metaphors; we don't necessarily see *is* in these phrases. In most cases, we also do not even see two terms from different semantic fields in these phrases. In preaching, these phrases naming concrete actions, places, or moments in time *become* metaphors as the preacher connects them (with an implicit *is*) to experiences familiar to listeners.

For example, in the sermon built on the very first phrase in the first list, the core affirmation[6] of the sermon was: "If we want to live in the way of Jesus in this world, we'll have to get our hands dirty." To take the final phrase from the *metaphors of place* list, a preacher began by telling the story of sitting for hours at his father's deathbed: "As my father faded, that stark room I had come to hate through

---

6. A sermon's *core affirmation* is the central affirmative statement it seeks to get across to its hearers (usually an affirmation about divine action in the world and the implications for human lives). See Sally A. Brown and Luke A. Powery, *Ways of the Word: Learning to Preach for Your Time and Place* (Minneapolis: Fortress, 2015), 125, 126, 142–52.

the weeks of his illness became holy ground." In the sermon, he went on to take his listeners (imaginatively) to a bitter-cold street corner where he and two homeless women waited for the light to change. All at once, one of the homeless women takes off her sweater and wraps it around the shoulders of the other. "We three stood on holy ground."

Metaphors of Action

we'll have to get our hands dirty
dance to a different drummer
marching off the map
lay down our swords
unlock the doors
going to the back of the line
getting low
stand your ground
border crossings

Metaphors of Place

between no place and someplace
under the bridge
off the map
the waiting room
the witness box
the last stop
where nobody knows your name
Ground Zero
holy ground

Metaphors of Time

eleventh hour
it's Friday, but Sunday's comin'
rush hour
the dark before the dawn
zero hour
unholy week
at an unexpected hour
moving day

Readers will be able to come up with far more phrases that refer to action, place, or time and that have metaphorical potential. Sometimes, good metaphors are ones known best to your congregation, because of their local character. I remember hearing a sermon where "the Harborside Diner" functioned as a symbol for extra-mile hospitality. The Harborside was known in town because of the kindness of the proprietor, who regularly fed a few of the oldest residents in town, long since unemployable, especially at the end of the month when their social-security checks were spent. Extending a "Harborside-Diner welcome" became a metaphor for action that foreshadows the coming reign of God.

How Metaphors of Action, Place, or Time Work in Preaching: Three Sermons

Next, we explore three sermons built on metaphor. The Reverend Dr. Martin Luther King Jr. mobilizes a metaphor of *time* ("it is midnight . . .")—although secondarily, he also lifts up a metaphor of *action* (knocking on a closed door). Homiletics professor Anna Carter Florence sets us down in a *place* charged with ethical demand and redemptive possibility ("at the river's edge"). Pastor and teacher Carlyle Fielding Stewart summons us into active participation in redemptive hope by means of a metaphor of action ("re-digging [neglected] wells").

> BUILDING THE SERMON AROUND A METAPHOR OF *TIME*:
> MARTIN LUTHER KING JR., "A KNOCK AT MIDNIGHT"[7]

King's well-known sermon "A Knock at Midnight" is based on the parable of the householder who runs to his neighbor at midnight to beg bread for needy guests (Luke 11:5-7). The sermon was preached over fifty years ago in Chicago, Illinois. It was August 1967. By that

---

7. Martin Luther King Jr., "A Knock at Midnight," in *Strength to Love* (Philadelphia: Fortress, 1963), 58-68. In the paragraphs that follow, page references from this sermon are given in parentheses in the text.

time, controversy over the war in Vietnam had drawn public attention away from the agenda of securing the civil rights movement's
gains. Pessimism about the true success of the civil rights struggle
was beginning to undermine much of the early hopefulness and
zeal of the movement.

King's metaphorical reframing of this critical moment in national
life is established in his very first paragraph, with the words, "It is
midnight in the parable; it is also midnight in our world, and the
darkness is so deep that we can hardly see which way to turn." Like
the chiming of a gong, the phrase "it is midnight" rings out again and
again as King develops a picture of the critical nature of the times:
"It is midnight within the social order . . . a dreary and frightening
midnight . . . midnight in man's external collective life . . . paral-
leled by midnight in his internal individual life. It is midnight in the
psychological order. . . . It is also midnight within the moral order"
(58–60). With his characteristic talent for vividly capturing social realities, King paints the depth of this midnight in its many dimensions.

Then suddenly, King shifts our attention from the midnight
darkness of our situation and asks us to listen: "As in the parable,
so in our world today, the deep darkness of midnight is interrupted
by the sound of a knock" (60). People are knocking on the door of
the church for bread of many kinds—but too often, says King, they
are disappointed. "Midnight," admits King, "is a confusing hour
when it is difficult to be faithful." Yet the witness of the church, particularly the black church, "encompassed by a staggering midnight,"
has been to believe and to declare "that morning will come," based
on "the faith that God is good and just. When one believes this, he
knows that the contradictions of life are neither final nor ultimate"
(66). King closes the sermon by calling to mind that midnight hour
when it seemed the voluntary carpool organized in Montgomery,
Alabama, would be declared illegal; if it were, the entire bus boycott
could be a failed strategy, the suffering and solidarity, the patient,
persistent knocking on the doors of justice in the long night of
protest all for naught. Then on the evening of November 13, 1956,
as King sat with the lawyers in the carpool hearing, a piece of paper
was handed to him: the Supreme Court had declared bus segrega-
tion unconstitutional.

Using metaphors of time and action—midnight and the persistent knocking of the oppressed for justice—King aligns Jesus's parable of hope-filled persistence, the 1956 crisis and breakthrough, and his hearers' present experience of flagging hope and failing vision, to challenge the spreading sense of stagnation with a fresh sense that for all its complexities and discouragements, the present hour is still the hour of divine redemptive action.

BUILDING THE SERMON AROUND A METAPHOR OF *PLACE*:
ANNA CARTER FLORENCE, "AT THE RIVER'S EDGE"[8]

Anna Carter Florence's deftly crafted sermon "At the River's Edge" is based on the Exodus story in which Pharaoh's daughter, down by the Nile for her bath, draws the pitch-covered basket carrying the infant Moses from the water. As the title suggests, an image of *location*, the river's edge, functions metaphorically in this sermon. It is the literal setting for the biblical story, yet it is by no means a location peculiar to the story or to the biblical world; it is where we live, also. It is under our feet. A secondary, closely related image of *action*—taking up the child borne on the waters—ties the sermon to an underlying theme of the convocation in which she was preaching: the social issue of society's response to its children. Florence begins with this theme: "You can tell a lot about a society by looking at its children. . . . [T]hey are spokespeople for our values, our choices, our circumstances, and our lifestyles" (172–73).

Florence does not immediately tell us the story we already know well, the familiar narrative of the baby in the basket on the river. Instead, she focuses on the location that will prove crucial for this sermon and the kinds of action that can be taken by those who find themselves in that spot: "What interests me about this passage is the action of the story itself, the characters who labor between right and wrong at the river's edge" (173). With this simple move, Flor-

---

8. Anna Carter Florence, "At the River's Edge," in *A Chorus of Witnesses: Model Sermons for Today's Preacher*, ed. Thomas G. Long and Cornelius Plantinga Jr. (Grand Rapids: Eerdmans, 1994), 172–78. In the paragraphs that follow, page references from this sermon are given in parentheses in the text.

ence has located her listeners, imaginatively, on the river's edge with Pharaoh's daughter and her entourage. What that young woman does on the river's edge matters—and what *we* do "on the river's edge" matters, too.

Most of Florence's listeners know the story of the baby Moses by heart. But with the skill of a master storyteller and preacher, Florence does not immediately tell that story as we might have expected; instead, she introduces another, contemporary story. It, too, takes place along a river. It, too, involves a child. Florence takes us to a scene in John Steinbeck's *The Grapes of Wrath*. At the height of a flood, a pregnant young woman caught in the starvation and poverty of life in the Great Depression gives birth to a stillborn child. Her uncle John places the dead infant in an apple box and then, instead of burying it in the earth, carries it to the swollen river and sets it afloat, bidding the dead child tell to the city downstream the story of suffering out of which it was birthed. Florence makes a slight but clear allusion to the biblical story when she asks, "If a starving migrant worker doesn't spark compassion in us, then will a baby in a box, or in a basket, floating down the river?" (175). This move also keeps the listener mindful that the river's edge, the place where you put things into the river, or spot them, is a place charged with ethical significance.

Only at this point does Florence take us to the biblical narrative itself. The telling moves briskly, studded with contemporary allusions ("down to the river for a swim," "the Hebrews . . . in their ghettoes"). Such details serve to interweave the biblical context with our own contemporary context of experience. Florence slows the action to focus on the moment at which Pharaoh's daughter must have identified with a mother who would take such care, laboring to construct a basket sturdy enough, comfortable enough, visible enough to give her baby a chance at life.

As the sermon moves toward its close, Florence deepens the metaphors of location and action—river's edge, and response to what the currents bring to our feet. Allowing the image of water to interact with allusions to related ideas of birth and labor, Florence declares that those who find themselves at the river's edge, confronted by the currents with a child whose thriving is denied by law, must labor in the throes of ethical decision. Even as Pharaoh's daughter must enter into "labor" for life, despite the forces arrayed against this child, we too must "labor" for life for such a child. The river's current is as forceful and relentless as the waters of birthing. What will we do with the children it carries to us, regardless of color, religion, or sexual orientation? The river cannot be stopped, and the child cannot be ignored: "Nothing we can do to stop the pain. Nothing we can do to push the baby back. We've got to reach in there and pick it up and say, 'You are my son. You are my daughter . . .'" (178).

River's edge, the current as unstoppable as birth, the cry that reaches our ears whether we want to hear or not: these images are lodged in the imaginations of those who will go into their Monday world and find themselves, metaphorically speaking, poised at the river's edge of ethical decision, compelled to decide and to act.

With characteristic skill, Florence weaves into this sermon not only a metaphor of place—the river's edge—but others as well: metaphors of action, including laboring, birthing, and dealing with a vulnerable child. These metaphors converge to reframe our own place, wherever we stand in life and in society, as a place of redemptive responsibility and possibility. *We* are at the river's edge. And whatever the river brings us, *we* are the agents whose turn it is to act.

> BUILDING THE SERMON AROUND A METAPHOR OF *ACTION*:
> "CAN YOU DIG IT?" BY CARLYLE FIELDING STEWART III[9]

Stewart's text for this sermon is Genesis 26:1–31. It tells the story of an episode in the life of Isaac. To escape famine, Isaac lives for a time among the Philistines, in the territory of King Abimelech. But eventually, Abimelech drives Isaac out, back to arid lands once occupied by his father Abraham. Back in the territory of promise, Isaac must face a risky challenge. He needs water. Should he attempt to dig out the old wells—Abraham's wells that are in the land already,

---

9. Carlyle Fielding Stewart III, "Can You Dig It?," in *Joy Songs, Trumpet Blasts, and Hallelujah Shouts: Sermons in the African-American Preaching Tradition* (Lima, OH: CSS, 1997), 65–72. In the paragraphs that follow, page references from this sermon are given in parentheses in the text.

long ago covered with earth by Abraham's enemies, who are still hostile to Isaac and his line?

Taking straight from the text the image of digging neglected and buried wells, despite adversity, Stewart aligns it with the current challenges of social, cultural, religious, and economic renewal that his community faces:

> The question for Isaac is: Can he dig the wells of hope, prosperity, and the restoration of his people's personhood and spirituality? . . . The question for us today is: *Will* we, the people of God, dig or not dig the wells of hope, deliverance, liberation, and transformation for our people? (65)

Stewart sustains this close identification between Isaac's situation and that of his listeners throughout the sermon, moving smoothly between the biblical text and the contemporary situation of African American communities.

For several paragraphs, Stewart fills in the biblical story for listeners, telling them how Isaac came to find himself faced with the challenge to re-dig these wells. Here and there in this telling of the biblical tale, Stewart makes allusions to the historical experience of black communities and families, who, like Isaac and his family, have experienced troubled times. The central image of re-digging old wells takes on greater depth and texture, thanks to Stewart's skilled interpolation of contemporary details in his telling of the biblical story.

With the narrative background vividly filled in and the biblical and contemporary settings set in a lively, dialectical relation with one another, Stewart's sermon moves forcefully forward through three moves: digging the wells of family reclamation, digging the wells of self-determination and dignity, and digging the wells of communal, spiritual preservation.

The lyric parallelism between "reclamation," "self-determination," and "preservation" is intentional, of course, rendering the sermon more memorable for both preacher and listener. But Stewart does not rely on these lyric parallels to carry the sermon home to the imagination of the listener. What lodges this sermon's claim and challenge in the imagination of listeners is the gritty, robust, and effort-demanding image of digging out buried wells that will yield life-sustaining water in an arid land.

Critical to this sermon's success is Stewart's ability to turn the well-digging metaphor loose in relation to present challenges his listeners recognize. (My italics signal some of the key phrases.)

> African Americans have something of positive value in their personal family histories which *can become the watering ground* for the revitalization of our communities. . . . Some traditional and ritual practices *we should unearth and preserve.* Some practices of abuse we should relinquish. . . . Can you dig . . . the well of familial reclamation? (69)

Next, after discussing the importance of not only familial reclamation, but also self-determination, for the African American future, Stewart takes up the well-digging image once again. This time, adopting a popular phrase of the 1960s ("Can you dig it?"), well-digging functions metaphorically to evoke the effort it will take for African American communities to lay claim to a future of well-being:

> Can you *dig the well* of self-reliance and empowerment? Can you *dig the wells* of independent analysis? Can you develop your own cognitive processes into transcendent judgment that allows you to rise on the wings of God to see your problems from on high? . . . Isaac was determined to influence his future. We as the people of God should be determined in *saving and reclaiming* our communities. *Can you dig it?* (71)

Throughout the sermon, Stewart reminds his listeners that Isaac dug amid opposition; his adversaries attempted to thwart the well-digging enterprise all along the way. This allows Stewart to work with the metaphor in a way that takes account of the fact that reopening neglected, life-giving wells of strong family and cultural tradition, self-determination, and spiritual strength will not be easy.

Wisely, Stewart does not abandon the metaphor at the close of the sermon to "explain" his point, as a less artful preacher might be tempted to do. Had he done so, the effect would have been to undercut the metaphor and retract it, instead of handing it on to the congregation to continue generating insight amid the realities of their weekday world (72). One can imagine the congregation leaving this worship service with a vivid image at work in their minds, ready to take on the heavy, gritty work of unearthing and opening up silted-over resources, for themselves and for their children.

Six Guiding Questions for Choosing a Central Metaphor

Clearly, sermons built skillfully around a central metaphor have the capacity to establish deep resonances between the biblical text, historical and literary settings and situations, and contemporary experience. It is neither necessary nor wise to attempt to find an anchoring metaphor for every sermon; preaching will be, and needs to be, far more diverse than that, as previous chapters have already suggested.

At the same time, every preacher can learn, with experience, to recognize metaphorical phrases that comport well with the biblical text and the sermon's aims. Sometimes, a metaphor is already embedded in the text itself, although that does not automatically mean that a metaphor-driven sermon is the only way, or even the best way on a given occasion, to preach.

Asking six simple questions before settling on a metaphor as the guiding thread of a sermon can make all the difference between sermons that create followable sight lines of hope and those that do not.

1. Is it simple?

An image to anchor a sermon needs to be straightforward and simple to understand. It will be verbally easy to express and easy for listeners to envision. If it is difficult to describe, or not readily recognizable in your context, it probably will not work. A usable metaphor will not require complex description or lengthy explanation.

2. Are the fields of meaning and experience mobilized by this metaphor commonplace enough for everyone in the pews to relate to it?

Metaphors that arise from obscure fields of experience are not helpful; it takes far too much time to establish enough familiarity with the field of specialization represented to make the metaphor worthwhile. A metaphor from the lingo of surfing, for example, may work with a few listeners—but it may not be cross-generational enough to work. Sports and fitness metaphors, in general, have more limited relevance out in the pews than many preachers imagine.

Metaphors drawn from common childhood experience can be helpful, not only because all of us have had a childhood, but because children in the congregation may also tune into them. But here, too, caution is in order: metaphors that assume all childhoods were happy, secure ones are *not* helpful; they may, in fact, rake up disturbing memories and deep pain for some. Working with a metaphor like "jumping into your father's arms" (besides being perhaps too glib to carry much theological weight) is not helpful for those who have not had a father, or whose only physical contact with the father they had was painful.

Metaphors from commonplace activities—finding one's way home, meeting the eyes of a stranger, opening a door without knowing what you'll find, rubbing shoulders with someone who is "other" (on a subway, for example, or in the checkout line)—may work, if they have not been overused. (If overused, they've become dead metaphors, able to generate little new insight.) Of course, what counts as commonplace varies from congregation to congregation. Agricultural images may be natural, familiar, and accessible to a rural congregation, but mystifying to urbanites.

3. Is it widely accessible to all kinds of people, not exclusionary?

Metaphors should be tested to see whether they tend to exclude some listeners on the basis of race, gender, marital status, socioeconomic status, sexual orientation, or class. For example, in the Chris-

tian canon, marriage functions as a metaphor for the relationship
of God to Israel, as well as Christ to the church. Yet preachers do
well to balance this metaphor with others—for example, the vine
and the vinedresser, which occurs in both testaments as well—so
that those who for some reason have difficulty identifying with the
marriage metaphor do not struggle to connect with the sermon.

Images from film or literature are a special case. If the story in
which the image functions can be briefly—*quite* briefly—summa-
rized, an image of action or setting from a novel, play, or film may
work. (Remember, for example, Florence's deft sketch of the scene
from Steinbeck's *The Grapes of Wrath* in which a man sends the
tiny coffin of his niece's stillborn child down the river.) But actions
embedded in complicated plots that take several minutes to explain
need to be set aside. That said, nearly every preacher I have heard or
read who handles metaphor well is a consistent reader. Many also
take in good films and are keen observers of human behavior. Keeping our imaginations well stocked with vivid visual images—which,
drawn alongside human experience, can function metaphorically—
is a basic discipline for good preaching.

4. Is the image related to the biblical text?

All of the images in the three sermons just discussed pass this test,
of course, because they are taken from the text itself. In King's sermon, the knock-at-midnight metaphor is drawn straight from the
text and aligns with (and illumines) the critical social situation
King is addressing. The crisis of critical, life-sustaining need in the
text and the desperation for life-and-future-sustaining change in
society match up. In Florence's sermon, the central metaphor is
also in the text itself. We, like Pharaoh's daughter, stand on the
river's edge, as the human beings and human dilemmas that the
river current brings to our feet, bidden or unbidden, demand our
response. Stewart's sermonic metaphor is anchored directly in the
story of Isaac re-digging the covered-over wells that once belonged
to his father, Abraham. The action itself, together with the sense
of building on the work of forebears that links the contemporary

African American community with this biblical text, makes this a powerful metaphor for Stewart's context and purpose. Neglected reservoirs of family strength, self-determination, and hope are as important to the present survival and future thriving of African American communities as was life-giving water in Abraham's time. Typically, the aptness of a textual metaphor to the occasion and context is something the preacher feels even before she or he has begun to articulate it.

It's not wrong to search for a fitting biblical metaphor, but a preacher always has to beware of trying to force an image to work. Let's say that the text of choice is David's conquest of the Philistine warrior, Goliath, with a slingshot. The preacher decides his metaphor is going to be "the perfect shot." He tells a story about the best basketball shot of his life and then goes on to carry that metaphor forward, finally circling back to the text to say that David "made the perfect shot." This doesn't quite work. Why not? It doesn't work because David's skill with a slingshot is not the point of the biblical story; the power of God enabling David to do the unthinkable is the point—and that hardly comports with the preacher's perfect basketball shot situation (many sports figures' claims about God being "on their team" notwithstanding).

One of the hardest things for a preacher to do is to let go of an image that doesn't pass these six tests. The preacher may feel that if only she explains enough, an awkward metaphor can be made to work. But listeners, instead of finding themselves in the luminous clearing where faithful imagination goes to work, find themselves instead in an impenetrable thicket. When we have to struggle to grasp the preacher's metaphor, it will not travel with us out of the pew, let alone out of the parking lot.

5. Is the image free of awkward associations?

Some years ago, I heard a Maundy Thursday sermon that set me pondering. The preacher, seeking to help us sense the intimacy and audacity of Jesus's act of washing his disciples' feet, told of the care she received, and the sense of being deeply loved that touched her, when her spouse would massage her feet at the end of a long day. There was a touching, rather detailed description of this ritual.

Yet, as well-intentioned as this personal disclosure was, the tension in the sanctuary during the sermon was palpable. If it had been the authentic discomfort of recognizing how truly human, intimate, and tactile the presence of the Word incarnate is for us, that would have been fine; but when a few folks cautiously talked about it later, it was clear that their discomfort had to do with feeling forced into an up-close encounter with a married couple's private affection, without having a choice in the matter. Embarrassment prevented the intended theological insight from getting through.

Or let's say that a preacher wants to build a sermon on Jesus's interaction with the two thieves on the cross, working with the metaphor "scandalous mercy." In an effort to give the metaphor vividness, he refers in his sermon to a local court case where a judge recently shortened the detention sentence of a local youth arrested for torturing dogs in his neighborhood. While the preacher may intend this as an example of restorative justice and a display of mercy, the mercilessness of the wrongdoing is so disturbing that it tears us away from the sermon itself. This judge's act of mercy cannot be surgically separated from the shocking nature of the offense; and the preacher will have to seek other examples.

6. Does the metaphor have semantic size, depth, and breadth?

This criterion is closely related to the one we have just discussed. The images we choose need to be "large" enough to help us envision the depth and breadth of both sin and redemption. The gestures, locations, and significant moments in time that we choose need not involve important, well-known figures; in fact, it is better if they do not. What they do need is *gravitas*—something that is, at the same time, utterly simple and deeply profound.

Standing on the riverbank, alert to see and hear what the river is bringing to our feet, is a powerful metaphor for ethical accountability. It is polyvalent, by which we mean that it can function in a variety of contexts, evoking different shades and levels of meaning as it is turned loose into different settings or situations. A good image for preaching has this quality of polyvalence.

Especially as you begin to work with metaphor-driven sermon designs, it's helpful to test your vision of the sermon with one or two trustworthy friends (or, better yet, fellow preachers) for theological weightiness, accessibility, and contextual appropriateness. Finally, once you feel confident in your metaphor-driven sermon, resist the temptation to get into the pulpit and introduce your metaphor as a kind of foreign object, to explain where you got it, and to defend it. None of this is necessary. This is like pausing at the beginning of the party you're throwing to defend the guest list and the menu. Trust the metaphor. Turn it loose. Let it do its work. Coupled with Scripture and recognizable scenes in human experience, a metaphor functioning throughout a sermon establishes its validity as it makes its way from your imagination to the imaginations of your listeners.

Turning Faithfully Improvisational Imagination Loose in the World

A metaphor at the heart of a sermon, biblical or drawn from human experience, sets up a semantic chemical reaction, an epistemological combustion. As it makes its way with each listener into the settings and situations of his or her everyday experience, new bursts of insight will disclose unseen possibilities and avenues of action in those spaces. These will far exceed the imagination of the preacher.

In other words, a strong metaphor is more than a connecting thread; it is portable wisdom, a powerful navigational tool. It will open sight lines of hope in the life of the congregation, as well as in the Monday-to-Saturday world unique to each listener.

Yet there is a caveat. While the strategies we've discussed in this chapter, and all the previous ones, are worthy and potentially helpful for our listeners, there is something else they are going to need, and we preachers can't grant it. They need the vision to discern on Monday the redemptive activity of God amid the often mundane tasks and demands of an ordinary life. They need, moreover, the stabilizing presence of the Spirit in an increasingly distressing, conflict-fraught world shredded by deep division and frantic self-aggrandizement fueled by toxic rhetoric and fears of the "other." These necessary gifts are not ours to give, but God's alone.

In other words, no homiletical strategy can substitute for the work of the Spirit. This fact functions as a sobering limit on our homiletical ambitions and as a profound comfort. Our part is not to say everything or fix everything. Our part is to step to the pulpit and practice and model a hermeneutic of hope; to fill the reservoirs of practice and storied wisdom; and to turn loose metaphorical sight lines of hope. That done, we can step back and trust that the Spirit is at work every day, turning ordinary believers in ordinary places into agents of redemptive hope, testifying in word and deed to the radical mercy, inclusive love, and restorative justice of God.

Index

Titles Published in

THE GOSPEL AND OUR CULTURE SERIES